The REAL WITCHES' CRAFT

The REAL WITCHES' CRAFT

Magical Techniques and Guidance for a Full Year of Practising the Craft

KATE WEST

HARPER
element

HarperElement
An Imprint of HarperCollins*Publishers*
77–85 Fulham Palace Road
Hammersmith, London W6 8JB

and *HarperElement* are trademarks of
HarperCollins*Publishers* Limited

First published by HarperElement 2005

© Kate West 2005

Text illustrations by Chris Down

Kate West asserts the moral right to
be identified as the author of this work

A catalogue record for this book
is available from the British Library

ISBN 0 00 719417 X

Printed in U.S.A

CONTENTS

This book is dedicated to my readers, without whom there would be no point, and also to all those who really do watch, listen, think, learn and grow in the ways of the Old Ones.

May you shine and grow, may you live in harmony with the land, and be at peace with yourselves. May you find love in those you love, and receive care from those you care for. May your wants be few and your rewards be many. And may you be ever free.

Blessed Be
Kate

Acknowledgements

My gratitude, as ever, to all my family and friends for their love and encouragement. To my fellow Witches and the Celt, for giving me the support I needed to keep on writing. Especially to all those who have truly supported and helped me, who have taken burdens from my shoulders, and worries from my brow. By now you should know who you are!

My thanks also to all those other authors whose writings have been a light on what, at times, has seemed an ever-darkening path and who, therefore, have given me a much needed impetus. To Terry Pratchett and the late Douglas Adams for reminding me of the shortcomings of reality, and to Bill Bryson for making some sense of it, and to Wendy Mewes for fine escapist Craft reading, which is much needed, and for a personal reminder that authors are real people too!

And my very, very, grateful thanks to Carole, my editor, and to Chris Down, the artist, for being so very patient and understanding.

MAKING
MAGIC WORK

The path of the Craft is as much a journey of self-exploration as it is a journey into other worlds, if not more so. To understand what lies around us we have to develop and refine our own self-knowledge and awareness. We need to put aside the limitations we learned through our formative years so that we can appreciate the skills and talents we truly have. It is only through a process of self-development that we can become who we're really capable of being, and thereby truly able to realize the magic we know we're capable of working to help ourselves and the world around us.

In the letters written to me by readers, and in conversations with those who come to hear me speak, I am often asked how to learn and develop the abilities which go to make magic and spells really effective; how to learn to meditate, visualize and so forth. I'm also asked why some spells never seem to come together or to actually work. These are the things which cannot just be read about; they have to be practised, over and again in order to develop our skills, even by experienced Witches. In a Coven, these are the skills which the High Priestess endeavours to develop in her Covenors, but many Witches today do not belong to a Coven, so this book is a guide to developing the techniques to make magic work.

Magic, as I have so often been heard to say, is not cookery. It is not simply assembling a series of ingredients and following a recipe from a book. Nor is it something which can be bought: no matter how much money you spend on books, tools, equipment, candles, crystals or whatever, it still will not enable you to create magical change. Neither is it a question of discovering special 'words of power', incantations, chants and so on, which will summon invisible aid to do your bidding. There is no quick route to learning how to create effective magic. Magic and, for that matter, the other aspects of Witchcraft, depend upon learning and practising certain skills and techniques. The good news is, however, that these skills are present to a lesser or greater extent in everyone, and the techniques to learn them are available to all; it just needs guidance, application, repetition and effort.

There are several keys to effective magic: The ability to control and balance the energies of the five Elements of Air, Fire, Water, Earth and Spirit that are within each of us. The ability to harness those energies as they are in the world around us and to focus and direct them in order to create the intended change. Knowledge and understanding of the ways those Elements manifest themselves in others. The ability to fully use the senses of sight, hearing, touch, taste and smell, to enable the development of the sixth, or psychic, sense. The knowledge this brings makes it possible to make magical change without unwanted side effects. The ability to develop and maintain focus and control in order to minimize the effort required. The ability to visualize, for it is true seeing of the magical intent which makes the magic happen. The ability to use one or more methods of divination which not only give the opportunity to see what might otherwise be hidden, but which also help to determine the potential consequences of our magical actions, and indeed whether they are necessary. An understanding of ways in which magic works and why it sometimes does not. Correctly identifying magical needs. The best use of the different tools and equipment to enhance magical intent. Ways of

the real witches' craft

designing the spells you cannot find in books. Creation of the Sacred Space for the working of magic at any time or place. Knowledge of the divine, the Goddess and the God, which is a key part of our Craft. Use of the Moon's phases to enhance magic and ways of turning the spell around when it cannot wait for the 'right' time. Ways of stopping and undoing spells, as well as methods of protection and defence. How to use the energies of the seasons to enhance magical work throughout the wheel of the Year.

This book examines all these aspects of the Craft, explaining how they contribute to the creation of magic, and giving techniques for developing and enhancing the required skills. Each chapter explores a skill and gives exercises to enhance your abilities. Some of these may appear simplistic, and some may appear to have little to do with the practice of Witchcraft, but when practised and mastered they come together to provide the techniques necessary to create effective magic and spell-craft. If you were working within a Coven, these would be the skills you would learn and practise in training sessions, enabling you to become an effective member of the magical team. To get the most out of these, take your time and go through them carefully.

Some you may have to repeat a few times, as these are skills you probably have not practised before. Think of it as being like exercising a new set of magical muscles. Most experienced Witches have their own versions of these kinds of exercises and practise them regularly, no matter how long they have been in the Craft. There is no reason why you should not continue your existing magical practices alongside these areas of study. If you do, you will notice an increasing effectiveness in the magic you work, as each of the abilities starts to take effect. A few of the exercises require certain conditions: phases of the Moon, a particular type of weather, and so on. It is up to you whether you pause in your study and wait for the appropriate conditions or whether you carry on and return to them at a later date. But do try to ensure that you cover them all.

Be aware that everyone is different and learns at a different rate. You may well find that some skills are easier or harder to master than others, and it may

making magic work

take several months to master a technique; if so, persevere, it will be worth it in the long run. You may also find that there are periods when you cannot devote as much time as you would like, or when you are tired, worried or just find it hard to focus. At these times you may want to pause and reflect on how far you have come, rather than pushing yourself further. You can always take a break and come back to your studies a few days or weeks later. The Craft will still be there when you are ready to go back to it.

I strongly recommend that you keep a record, or journal, of your magical practice, often called a Book of Shadows. Make notes of what you did, what you hoped would happen, and what the actual results were. Remember to include information on the phase of the Moon, and on your feelings before, during and after your workings. Not only will this provide you with a record of your progress and help you to determine what works for you and what doesn't, but later you will find it an invaluable record of which spells are most effective in themselves.

Whilst this book is written in chapters which allow you to practise each technique separately, there is an element whereby you may find that it is only after you have worked through the whole that you can really appreciate the individual components and the contribution they make to your practice of the Craft.

We are so used to the promised quick-fix solutions to the problems of life, from TV instant makeovers to self-help books which promise to turn our lives around in a week, that we have forgotten that it takes time and effort to achieve really worthwhile skills. Some people ask me why I don't just write down the 'hidden secrets' of Witchcraft. The problem with this is that such 'secrets' are those same skills which take time and practice to learn. The Craft is not, and will never be, a quick-fix. Just as the 'inner secrets' of the Craft are the achievement of balance and control over ourselves, which enable us to utilize the energies within and without, there is no such thing as 'advanced spells'; there are only advanced Witches whose spells really work.

the real witches' craft

Of course, Witchcraft is not just about spells and magic, although these factors are the most obvious difference between this and other belief systems. Throughout this book I have also endeavoured to touch upon the other elements of the Craft which all go towards the making of a Witch.

One of the things I have noticed as I write books on the Craft is that each layer of questions I answer reveals yet another layer of questions. Not that this is unexpected, for it's an inherent part of the Craft that the more you know, the more you find that there is to know. But it does indicate that whilst, by the time you get to the end of this book, it will have answered some of your questions it will also, if it does its job, give you another set of things to think about and more questions to ask.

So, if you would seek some answers, and some new, better and far more interesting questions, read on.

Blessed Be
Kate

Chapter One

ELEMENTS:

The Cornerstones of Magic

Knowledge and understanding of the Elements underlies the whole of the Craft and is essential to the creation of effective magic. Almost every aspect of the Craft relates back to the Elements in one way or another. Whilst it is possible to work some spells without a thorough understanding of them, such spells are generally less effective and often do not work accurately, or even at all.

The Elements we refer to in the Craft are not those of the periodic table but the basic attributes or forces of nature and the land. They are Air, Fire, Water, Earth and Spirit. In their various forms these are the aspects of nature from which all life comes and which affect all aspects of our whole existence.

Air is the wind, from the gentlest summer breeze to hurricanes and tornados which can devastate the earth. All living things need air, in one form or another, to breathe. **Fire** is the heat and light of the Sun, as well as the flames which can be sparked to bring light into our homes, or to run wild and burn all in their path as in the forest fire. All life needs light and heat, to a greater or lesser degree, to survive. **Water** is everything from a gentle shower to the heavy rain, as well as streams, rivers, oceans and seas, whether still or in the grip of a great storm. At its most savage it is the tsunami or tidal wave which sweeps all before it. Again all life forms require water for survival. **Earth** is the rocks, stones, pebbles and crystals as well as the soil from which things grow; it is also the earthquake which can erase all life. It is the medium in which the plants grow, which form the basis of the food chain. **Spirit** is the mysterious and divine spark of life, the difference between something which lives, grows and reproduces, or which lies still and inert.

This chapter will focus primarily on the four Elements of Air, Fire, Water and Earth. To ancient mankind these Elements were the things which influenced and controlled every aspect of daily life, which determined whether there was enough to eat and whether the people prospered or not. These Elements could bring plenty or famine, give or take life. Indeed they still can and do, you only have to watch the news to see the effects of hurricanes, forest fires, drought, famine, earthquakes, landslides, tsunamis and other results of too much or too little of any of the Elements. The fifth Element, Spirit, is the difference between things living and things not, and is also the Divine, the Goddess and the God. The chapter on Spirit focuses on the Goddesses and Gods and on ways of developing your understanding of them. In the meantime, when called upon to do so, visualize them in whichever way feels most comfortable to you.

In the Craft, and some other belief systems, the Elements are not only physical forces in nature, they are also a part of us. Air is our thoughts, that part of us which thinks; it is also our breathing and the sense of smell. Fire is our passions and enthusiasms, those strong feelings which can take over and make us act or react. It is the beat of the heart and the sense of sight. Water is our emotions, joy and laughter, sorrow and tears. It is the blood that runs through our veins and the sense of taste. Earth is our physical form, the body, and the sense of touch. Spirit is that intangible part of us which can be called the sense of self or soul.

The Elements are also present in, and linked to, other aspects of life; time of day, season of year, age of a person, and direction of the compass. Air, which should always come first, both represents and is represented by morning, spring, youth, and the East. Fire is the afternoon, summer, adulthood and the South. Water is evening, autumn, middle age and the West. Earth is night, winter, age and the North. Spirit encompasses them all. The Elements are also a part of everything we do in ordinary life. Air is the idea and thinking process. This is the reason why Air is first, for thought should always precede and lead to any action. Fire is the enthusiasm which makes us want to put thought into action. Water is our emotional involvement. Earth is the actual physical making it happen. Spirit is the spark which brings it all to life, the part of our inner self which we give to make it special and 'our own'.

The Elements are also the foundation of the Witches' Circle. Each is called, invoked or summoned to attend, and each is assigned the quarter which relates to its compass point; i.e. Air in the East, Fire in the South, Water in the West and Earth in the North. Spirit is both the Goddess and the God, and the self, it is also both the centre of the Circle and its whole. We also use colours to represent the Elements: yellow for Air; red for Fire; blue for Water, and green for Earth. However, other colour combinations are sometimes used. To craft an effective spell we must firstly have the idea (Air), we need to be enthusiastic about it (Fire), we become emotionally involved with it (Water), and then we put it into action (Earth), but we must also add a bit of our inner self (Spirit) to make it happen.

These attributes of the Elements show how important they are in both life and the Craft, for not only are they powerful forces of nature but they also pervade every part of our lives and our inner being. To create effective magic it is essential that we get to know and understand the Elements and everything they link to. To make that magic work the way we want it to, we have to be able to harness their energies both from inside us and from outside. The first step towards this is to actually experience the Elements in nature.

elements: the cornerstones of magic

PRACTICAL WORK 1

Take time out to experience each of the Elements in its natural state in turn. Be prepared to spend a little time on each; at least 15 minutes, preferably more. Do not be tempted to try to deal with more than one Element on any one day. As these exercises really must take place outdoors, please make sure that you pay attention to your personal safety. If you can, remove your footwear so that you are in direct contact with the earth. Also experiment with having your eyes open and closed. Try to use all of your senses: sight, hearing, touch, smell and taste. In the case of the latter, you may find it better to inhale through your mouth rather than, for example, actually placing soil into it. Pay attention to how each Element makes you feel both physically and emotionally.

Air – On a windy day, go to a high point, preferably one which is not sheltered by trees or buildings, where you can experience the Element of Air. If it is cold, make sure you wrap up well. Feel the air blowing through your hair, moving your clothes and trying to buffet you. Take with you a few leaves or flower petals and cast them into the wind, watching how it takes them, lifts them and moves them. As you stand there, give thought to other types of winds, both stronger and gentler.

Fire – On a hot and/or sunny day go to somewhere which is sheltered from the wind, where you can lie down in the sunlight. Absorb the heat and light of the Sun, feeling also the warmth of the land you are lying on. Take your time to think about all the things which depend upon heat and light, but do not risk sunburn or look at the Sun itself. Imagine what life might feel like with much less, or much more, Sun.

Water – Here are two ways of experiencing Water; do both if you possibly can so that you can compare the experiences. First, go out in the rain, lift your head up and catch some drops in your mouth. Allow the rain to wash over you, look at the ways it lands upon trees and plants and the way it soaks into the earth. Also observe the way it behaves when it lands on the pathway or road, and look at the effects it has on the things around. Whilst you are there, consider the benefits of the rain. Secondly, go to a stream, river, pond or lake which is not too dirty or polluted. Put your naked feet into the water, and use your hands to splash a little onto your face. Again, give thought to life with much less or more water, and consider those parts of the world where all the water is frozen as well as those where water is scarce. If you live near the coast, then also do the second part of the exercise in the sea, perhaps even going right into the water and submerging yourself completely if it is safe to do so.

Earth – The first part of this exercise is best undertaken in your own garden, or in that of someone who is prepared to let you actually dig the earth. If neither is possible then you can use a tub or container of earth as an interim measure, but do try to return to the Element at some point. Dig a hole wide enough for you to place both hands in it, and deep enough that you actually go beneath the top 2–3 inches. As you dig, look carefully at the things within the soil, both living and inanimate. Use your hands to feel the texture, both on the surface and further down. If you can, place your feet into the earth too. The second part may be something you have to defer until you go on a trip to somewhere suitable. Find some rock formations – they don't need to be huge or particularly impressive. Place your hands flat on the rock surface. Look at the stone to see what is growing there, noting colour, texture and the direction of any lines and cracks. Consider the forces and energies that resulted in their being. If you have the chance, try also to visit a cave so that you can also experience being surrounded by the earth.

When you return home after each experience, make sure that you write it up, including all the thoughts and feelings that came to you whilst experiencing each Element.

You may find it helpful to start a new page or section of your journal for each Element, as this is only the first of several exercises on the Elements and you may wish to group all those relating to each Element together. As you go to sleep on the night of your experience, make a real effort to recall all those thoughts and feelings. If you dream of the Element you might also like to write this up.

Once you have given yourself the chance to really feel the Elements in nature you may find that you begin to feel differently about them. For example, attempting to appreciate the part that Air and Water play in the cycle of life makes it easier to understand the need for rain and storms and hence make it easier to accept 'bad' weather. You may also find that you enjoy being out in the Elements in a more meaningful way. Many Witches make a point of regularly taking the time to enjoy the experience of the Elements as they can actually draw energy from them.

Following on from the experience of the Elements in nature you need to get to really know them within. As mentioned before, each Element has its counterpart in ourselves: Air is thought, Fire is passion, Water is emotion and Earth is our physical being. It is important that we get to know how the Elements are working within us as this colours our feelings, the way we behave in life and

the real witches' craft

react to others. If Air, or thought, is dominant, then we may spend too much time in abstract thought and nothing will get done. If Fire, or passion, is emphasized then we may find that we react without considering the consequences; anger or passionate love, for example, can make us do things which we subsequently regret! When Water, our emotions, dominate then we can be easily moved to tears or laughter, even though it may not be a good time or place. And being overly focused on the physical realm, or Earth, can easily result in not being able to focus or concentrate on anything else, in the same way that a bad toothache can make it impossible to attend to almost anything else.

Because the energies of the Elements are the key to working magic then it is important that we really understand our internal Elemental balance. Any imbalance will have to be addressed before we can work magic, otherwise the results may not be what we intended. Working magic when Air is dominant can result in spending all your energy on going over the problem but little personal involvement. Of course, if Air is absent, then the spell will not be thought through or may be misdirected. If Fire is dominant then there is the risk that a spell may be fired off in anger, and regretted later! If Fire is absent then you are unlikely to have the strength of feeling to actually put the magic into action. Where emotions are high, and Water is dominant, it is hard to focus on anything and your spell will almost certainly come to nothing, if indeed you actually complete it. Where the emotions are not involved then there will be no feeling. When Earth is over-emphasized then there is a tendency to expend all your energy on the physical bits and bobs which come with magic, like the tools, candles, etc rather than actually making the magic work. Without Earth then it is unlikely you will even get around to doing anything. This understanding of the way we really feel would be a lot easier if we were all truly in touch with ourselves all of the time. However, once we leave early childhood we are all taught to reign in our feelings, not to show anger or weep open tears. We even learn to suppress some of our physical needs; not eating because it is not the 'right' time, concealing discomfort to wear fashionable or 'correct' clothing, etc. For these reasons it is important to spend time learning how to get to know our inner feelings as they really are, rather than the way we hope they are.

PRACTICAL WORK 2

During parts of the following exercises you may access some fairly strong feelings, so before you begin it is a good idea to make sure you are prepared to deal with these and are able to bring yourself back to 'normal'. In the Craft we sometimes call this returning to ourselves 'grounding' or 'earthing', and it is something which should take place after any kind of meditation, as well as any form of magical working. Probably the best way to ground yourself is to have a warm drink and something to eat, preferably sweet, to replenish your physical energy as well. Alternatives include briskly rubbing your arms and legs with your hands, or fairly strenuous but tedious physical activity such as doing the vacuuming!

Dealing with strong emotions can be somewhat harder, and often it is best to allow them to work themselves through; if you feel like crying then do so, if you feel anger then go and pummel a pillow or cushion, and so on. Because these exercises can arouse strong feelings you may want to ensure that you will have privacy both during and afterwards. Part of the object is to learn how to handle your feelings, so please don't try to suppress them. On the other hand, many people find that they have no residual effects after the experiences, and this, too, is perfectly normal. As with the preceding exercises only try to deal with one Element on any one day and write it up as soon as you can.

the real witches' craft

Air – In some respects, deliberately bringing the Element of Air, and thought, to the fore is the hardest to achieve; as it is hard to think, and think about how you are thinking, at the same time. Because of this here is a selection of exercises you can choose from:

- ❦ Imagine you are going away for a few days. Try to choose somewhere particular but which you have not visited before. Take a pen and paper and make a list of everything you think you might need to take with you. Plan for every situation, event and weather you can sensibly imagine happening. Be as detailed and thorough as you possibly can. When your list is finished, make a second list, this time assuming you can only take one very small bag. When both are complete, compare the way you felt whilst compiling each.
- ❦ In your head, calculate the number of seconds in a year or, if you find this easy, the number of seconds you have been alive.
- ❦ Imagine a conversation with someone you know fairly well, but make it about a subject neither of you knows a lot about. Try to imagine what each of you will say, and make it last for at least ten minutes.

Afterwards, consider how it felt to be strictly focused on mental activity: were you at all aware of your body, or other aspects of yourself?

Fire – If you have a real fire then this is best, otherwise place several candles in front of a mirror so that you can see lots of flames. Do make sure that they are in secure holders and not likely to set the room on fire! Now recall a time when you were really very angry – anger is often the easiest passion to recall. Think through the whole situation from the first things that upset you until you can really feel the anger rising up inside of you. Once you are truly angry, stop for a moment and think about how your whole body and mind feel. You may find that you are shaking, sweating or have other physical symptoms. If another person was the cause of this anger, ask yourself how you would feel about working a healing spell for that person right now. Once you have explored the sensations, either work through the feeling or let it subside naturally. Make notes on the build-up of feelings, how you felt when they were at their most powerful and how you felt as they were released or subsided.

Water – To explore your emotions do both parts of this exercise: In the first part run yourself a deep, pleasantly warm bath. Make sure that you have a specially warm and fluffy towel to hand for afterwards, and a box of tissues within reach just in case. Once you are in the water think back to an event which was particularly sad; perhaps the loss of a pet, or the break-up of a relationship. Again, allow yourself to really experience the feelings that made up the emotion. Write this up fully as before.

Do the second part on a separate occasion: Choose a humorous book to read or film to watch, making sure it is something which will really make you laugh out loud; often this will be something you are already familiar with. Alternatively, recall a really funny situation that happened to you, or which you have heard about. Allow the humour to build, and afterwards give thought to how you felt. When you write this up, compare it with experiencing sadness and see what, if anything, you feel the build-up of the two emotions have in common, and what is different about each. Also compare the way they leave you feeling once they have subsided.

Earth – This exercise is one which may take several attempts to complete, as lots of people fall asleep when first trying. It is, however, something you might like to repeat many times as it is very relaxing. Prepare for bed in the usual way: if you are in a relationship you may need to have an early night when your partner will join you later. Lie on your back with no pillows under your head. Try to ensure you are lying

the real witches' craft

straight with your feet slightly apart and your arms beside you but not touching your sides. Focus on your breath until you are breathing slowly and evenly in through your nose and out through your mouth. Now, starting with one foot, move one toe at a time, then stretch and flex the foot. Do the same with the other foot. If you can't actually move your toes one at a time, do your best. Now flex the ankles one at a time, then rotate them. Going slowly up your body, bend and flex each muscle group or joint as best you can. Continue right up to moving your neck, chin, mouth, eyes, eyelids and eyebrows. If you are still awake, repeat the process in reverse. When you have finished, your whole body should feel completely relaxed. Lie there for a few moments and think about how each part of your body felt before, during and after you moved it. Imagine your mind travelling through all the parts and try to see them in your imagination. Ask yourself how they really feel: are there any aches, pains or discomforts? Which parts feel good, which don't? The following day, and only after you have written up the first part, stand naked in front of a mirror and make a point of looking at all the parts of your body. Compare how you feel about the way each looks, with how they actually felt in the movement exercise.

The above exercises allow you to explore your feelings in association with the Elements in an experimental way, but this is somewhat artificial as it relates to feelings you have deliberately summoned and, to a certain extent, controlled. In daily life things are not usually quite so straightforward. During the course of any one day you will go through a lot of different feelings; some quite mild, some stronger. You will also have mixes of feelings; for example, someone makes you a bit angry (Fire), but because you are not allowed to show that, you also feel frustrated (Water). It is important that you learn to recognize the more subtle feelings, and their different combinations, as this enables you to take the appropriate corrective action before starting magical work. To gain a better understanding of how the Elements affect you it is a good idea to keep a record of your feelings for a short while.

PRACTICAL WORK 3

The Element Diary – For at least one week, keep a detailed record of your feelings, linking them with their associated Elements. Make entries for first thing on waking, mid-morning, lunchtime, mid-afternoon, early evening, and last thing at night. You may also find it helpful to note any triggers you can identify which may have brought on these feelings.

After just a week of this you will already have a far greater understanding of the ways the Elements work in your life. You will also find that you start to have far more control over the ways you react to people and events around you. One of the effects of this is that you can begin to avoid situations, and sometimes even the people, which affect you badly. The next stage is to begin to find ways of effectively dealing with your feelings. Not by suppressing them but by balancing them.

The first step towards this is to find simple, easy to recall images which, for you, instantly identify each Element. For some people this means remembering the Elements as they actually experienced them in nature, for others it can be visualizing the colours. I have a series of mental 'video clips'; time-lapse images of clouds rushing across the sky, a volcano erupting, waves crashing on the shore, and a cliff face I used to visit often. Whatever your personal triggers, when you recall them they should immediately invoke each Element totally; in terms of all the senses, as well as the internal feelings of each. If you don't already have a series of memorable images then spend some time working on them. One Witch I know spent time creating abstract pictures of each. She made these pictures close to the Elements in nature; on a hill, in the sun, by a stream and in the garden surrounded by freshly turned earth. Whilst drawing her pictures she focused on all the aspects of each Element, revisiting the feelings, sights, sounds, smells, etc of each, and she dedicated them to each Element. The effort she put into these images was well worth it, as every time she wants to recall them they come easily to mind. Another, who is a singer, worked on finding musical tones which bring the Elements immediately to mind. Once you have decided which form is best for you, practise it regularly until you can recall each Element fully whenever you want.

After this you will need to identify ways of sending them away with equal ease. For a mental picture you might imagine a particular Element fading until it is no longer visible, or see it being covered by a coat of 'paint' which causes it to disappear. Sounds can be imagined as getting quieter, and so on.

PRACTICAL WORK 4

Find and develop mental images which bring to mind each of the Elements in turn. Keep practising until you can hold the images of all the Elements at the same time. Don't expect to actually 'see' all four at the same time, but you should be able to maintain the feeling that they are all present. When you are able to bring them all to mind with ease, and hold them in your mind at the same time, then work on a way of sending each away, just as effectively.

Once you have mastered this, you can start to apply this technique to balance the Elements within. Continue using your Element Diary, but this time, every time you note a feeling, take a moment to recall each of your Elemental images in order. Whatever your feelings, bring to mind your images of Air, Fire, Water and Earth in that order. When you have all four in mind, revisit the images, but this time make each fade in your mind. Remember to note down how effective this was in reducing your feelings and balancing the Elements within.

It is very unusual for this technique to be effective straight away, and most Witches find that they have to practise over and over to achieve it fully. Moreover, there may well be times when your feelings are so strong that you find the exercise almost impossible to carry out. Don't worry, this does not mean you have failed, but it does indicate that there are times when our feelings are so strong that it would not be a good idea to work magic. In fact, you should not attempt to work magic if you cannot achieve a balance in the Elements, as this will directly affect the results of your spell. If you are angry, even if it is unrelated to the spell you are working, then Fire will be in the ascendant and you may not give enough thought to constructing your spell. Likewise, if you are ill you may not be able to judge your Elemental balance accurately, let alone achieve focus and control.

Getting to grips with the Elements within can be used to give an insight into the ways others behave, and how they may react to life. If you observe those around you, you can often tell which Element(s) is (are) influencing their actions, and in some people which Elements they allow to control most of their lives. Some people are so Air-based that their life is all thinking and planning, with little actually getting done. These are the people you find need constant reminders and are not very practical. With others it may be Water, and they lurch from one emotional crisis to another. Fiery people are impulsive and often start many things, finishing few of them. Earth-based individuals are often practical but can seem cool and unemotional. This is one of the ways that those who are interested in Astrology use to guess the 'star sign' of people they meet, as all the signs are linked to the four Elements. Gemini, Libra and Aquarius are Air signs. Aries, Leo and Sagittarius are Fire signs. Cancer, Scorpio and Pisces are Water. Taurus, Virgo and Capricorn are Earth. However, in Astrology, as in the real world, few people are that uncomplicated, so they will often be influenced by more than one Element at a time, and can have different influences at different times. The observation and understanding of those around us is one of the key skills of the Witch, as it helps us to choose the best kinds of spell to achieve the desired effect.

PRACTICAL WORK 5

Give some thought to those around you. Which Elements are they most closely associated with? Try not to make it obvious that you are studying them; it will make them uncomfortable around you and is a good way to spoil relationships! Also, give some thought as to how this might affect the way you deal with them. For example, if you are seeking a favour from someone who is very Air-based, then it might be best to give a well thought out reason why they should help. But if they are Water-based then you could consider giving emotional reasons, and so on. If you experiment in this way, remember to make notes both before and after to see if your assessment of others is effective, and to help you develop your skills.

Of course, the effects of the Elements are not just limited to people; everything in the world is linked either to them or by them. Remember, they link to the times of day, the seasons, and even the ages of mankind. Hence, you can feel, and use, their influences in everything you do. If you need to plan something, then you might want to invoke Air. Conversely, if you are in need of rest, then you might want to bring Earth influences into your life.

In the Craft, the Elements are the corner-stones of the Circle, as well as of any magic or spells we may work. The Circle is on the one hand our Sacred Space, as a church or temple might be in other beliefs. But it is more than just a place to work. Its creation actually contributes directly to the actions which take place within it, as well as having specific purposes connected to the working of magic. It provides a protected area for all magical workings, where other, possibly negative energies, or just distractions, cannot enter. It contains the magical energy we raise to make the magic work, until the time when we release it to send it to its destination. Above all, it actually brings together the five Elements in such a way that we can add their energies from around us to those that we bring from within ourselves.

CREATING THE SACRED SPACE

Whether you are one person working alone, or a group, it is worth learning how to create the Sacred Space in a fairly formal way first, in order to understand how it works. First, an area, whether indoors or out, needs to be cleared, so that you can easily move around in it. It need not be large, but should have enough space to comfortably fit the person or people working within it, as well as any tools and equipment they may want or need to use. The traditional Circle is nine feet in diameter, but you may not have the luxury of that much room. The space will usually contain an Altar, which may be simply a table or surface onto which you put the things you will be using. If you are working indoors, this will include items to represent each of the Elements; incense for Air, a candle for Fire, a dish of water for Water and salt for Earth. The Goddess and the God may be represented by images, candles or other items. Visual links of this kind are more important in group working than they are when you work on your own, as everyone has to be focused on the same thing at the same time. If you are working magic which is going to centre around candles, a talisman or other physical objects, then these too should be on the Altar so that you do not later need to leave the Sacred Space to fetch anything.

First, stand in the East of your area, facing the East, and holding firmly in your mind the image of Air that you developed earlier, call on the Element saying:

'I call upon the Element of Air, to join with me here in the Circle.'

When you can actually feel the presence of Air, say:

'Blessed Be.'

Now move to the South of the area and repeat the process and words for the Element of Fire. In the West call upon Water, and in the North call upon Earth. In many groups the words will be accompanied by drawing the invoking pentagram, the five-pointed star, of each Element in the Air. Remain facing the North and call upon the Goddess and the God saying:

'I do call upon the Goddess and the God to join with me in these my Rites.'

Visualize them coming from the North to be with you and when you feel their presence say:

'Blessed Be.'

If you have preferred deity forms then you can name and visualize these; there is more on this later in the book. Lastly, move to the North-East of the Circle and with the forefinger of your strong hand draw a circle in the air around the outer boundary of the Circle. As you do so, visualize an electric blue light creating a circle which becomes a sphere containing the whole circle, and say:

the real witches' craft

'I do cast this Circle as a place of containment and protection. A place between the worlds and a time outside of time.'

Make sure that you overlap the start and finish points of the circle and then say:

'Blessed Be.'

Note that you should always move Deosil; that is clockwise, when creating and working in the Circle.

Your Sacred Space is now complete and ready for you to perform whichever magical action you need. Usually, this will include raising energy, the spell or magic, and celebrating the Rite of Wine and Cakes, all of which are covered later in this book. At the end of magical working you then need to dismiss the Elements and thank the Goddess and the God.

Again, start in the East of your area, facing the East, and holding firmly in your mind the image of Air that you developed earlier, call on the Element saying:

'I give thanks to the Element of Air, for joining with me here in the Circle. Hale and farewell.'

Let the image fade in the way you practised earlier, and when you feel it has departed, say:

'Blessed Be.'

Now move to the South of the area and repeat the process and words for the Element of Fire. In the West dismiss Water, and in the North, Earth. In many groups the words will be accompanied by drawing the banishing pentagram of each Element. Remain facing the North and call upon the Goddess and the God, saying:

'I give thanks to the Goddess and the God for being present here with me in these my Rites. Hale and farewell.'

Visualize them returning to the North and say:

'Blessed Be.'

Lastly, move to the North-East of the Circle and with the forefinger of your strong hand draw a circle in the air around the outer boundary of the Circle. This time visualize the electric blue sphere fading and dissipating, and say:

'I remove this Circle and return this place as it was before.'

Make sure that you overlap the start and finish points of the circle and then say:

'Blessed Be.'

You can also return the area, perhaps replacing furniture and so on, to its original state. Lastly, have something to eat and drink to ground yourself, and write up your journal, leaving space for any outcomes to be added later.

the real witches' craft

Learning and practising this way of creating, and later removing, the Sacred Space is a good way of finding out how it feels, even though you may choose to use a less formal way for most of your magical working. Obviously, not all spells can wait until you have the time and space for a formal circle. Sometimes you may have an urgent need to work magic when you are not at home, or alone, and you can hardly start clearing an area and reciting invocations in a busy public place! On these occasions you can work completely within your head, summoning each Element, inviting the Goddess and the God, and drawing the Circle, all without moving or speaking aloud. There is more on this later.

elements: the cornerstones of magic

PRACTICAL WORK 6

Practise formal invocations of the Elements. Remember to banish each, every time you call upon it, even if you do not think you were successful. You do not want even traces of Elemental energies hanging around. I have heard of cases when an Element has not been banished, resulting in burst pipes or an overflowing bath (Water), or electrical faults (Fire), and so on. Alongside this, practise bringing forward only your internal images of them, so that you can compare the way both forms of invocation feel. Aim to give your mental images the same energy as the more complex invocations. And, of course, note down your feelings regarding each technique.

The more you practise this the easier it will become, until you reach a point where all four can be brought to mind at will, taking only a little longer than it does to think of each in turn. This not only goes towards enabling you to work effective magic virtually anytime or anywhere, but it can also be used to balance yourself in daily life. Most of us have times when a dominant feeling or emotion affects the way we behave; for example, an argument at home can leave us angry, upset or confused, all feelings which are not helpful at work. Or someone else's inconsiderate driving may leave you cross and irritable, feelings which you don't want to take home to your family. If we can achieve balance we can put those feelings aside and behave in a way appropriate to the people around us, rather than taking out our frustrations on them. One of the ways of doing this is by taking a few moments to invoke and then banish the Elements. Of course, you may need to find a few moments of privacy to do this, but even a toilet cubicle should provide you with a little peace and quiet!

the real witches' craft

PRACTICAL WORK 7

Whenever you experience a strong feeling which is inappropriate to the setting you are in, make a point of invoking and banishing each of the four Elements. After you have done this, also take a moment to thank the Goddess and the God for their help. As with the other exercises, write this up as soon as you can.

It is important to remember to use this technique at the right time. You do not need to suppress feelings which are appropriate to the problem and in the appropriate setting. For example, if you are short-changed in a shop then it is right to point this out and to summon the manager if you do not get satisfaction. But if you feel that this is the 'last straw' in a day full of niggling aggravations, it is not right to berate the assistant as your first action. Use the balancing before making your point, whatever it be, calmly and sensibly, rather than explosively. Don't use it to suppress perfectly reasonable comments.

In some Covens knowledge of the Elements is taken very seriously and new members are set specific 'tests of the Elements' as a part of their early training. These can involve such things as visiting an underground cave and having the lights turned out, to gain a better appreciation of the sensation of Earth. Or total immersion in the sea for Water. In other groups, individuals are encouraged to set themselves their own 'tests' and to report back on what they did and how they reacted. Certainly, it is worth taking any opportunity to increase your understanding of the Elements. Some of the more 'extreme' ways include: taking a hot air balloon ride; attending a well-organized fire walking and have a go; taking an underwater swimming class; and getting a trusted friend to cover you up to the neck in a layer of pebbles on a stony beach. Of course, you can also think up your own. If, like many, you have a concern or fear about any particular Element, you will also find that is the experience you will gain most from. Having said that, please do observe safety considerations and don't take unnecessary risks.

Having worked through the above exercises you may want to work the Elemental Ritual near the end of this chapter. Of course, you could also work this Ritual at any full Moon, but it will be more effective if you have done the preparatory work. It gives you the opportunity to gain a greater experience of one of the four Elements and, if you haven't done so before, to create the Sacred Space. You can also revisit later to work with each of the other Elements. It can be worked by one person on their own, or by several people together if you prefer. It centres on contacting one of the kinds of Elemental being.

The Elemental Beings, or Elementals, are the 'life-forms', or creatures, made directly of the Elements. Sylphs are the creatures of the Air. Salamanders are those of Fire. Undines are the creatures of Water, and Gnomes the creatures of Earth. Try not to confuse these with their fairy-tale counterparts who are often depicted as being cute beings akin to the fairies of childhood. Remember that they are not only made of their representative Elements but that they are capable of being the extremes of those Elements. They should not be invoked casually, but should be treated with respect and should always be thanked, whether or not you feel you succeeded.

To try to contact any of the Elemental beings you need to create the right environment for their presence. Burning an appropriate incense can also help to attract them. In each case it is a good idea to spend a short amount of time focusing all your thoughts on the Element in question, and perhaps to review your notes on some of the preceding exercises so that you can immerse your mind in thoughts of the Element. Then, when you are truly ready to concentrate, you will be set to try to detect the Elemental in question.

the real witches' craft

Sylphs are the beings of the Air. They are light and are in fact around us all the time, however their presence can usually only be detected in smoke or mist, as it is their moving of the medium which is observed rather than their actual forms. When the smoke from incense moves without a draft or other movement in the room, this is the action of Sylphs. They are most easily attracted to light scents such as Jasmine and Lavender, and to the scents of seasonal flowers. As they dance and play in the winds, your invocation is more likely to succeed on a day when there is only the lightest of breezes, and they prefer an atmosphere which is warm and moist.

Salamanders are the beings of Fire. They can be seen dancing in the flames of a candle or a fire. If you have an open fire then there will almost certainly be salamanders there. They can be attracted to the flame of a red candle, and when the air is completely still you can see them move the flame. They require conditions which are hot and dry. It can also help to burn incense of rose or lotus. Note that these Salamanders are not the same as the lizards of the same name!

Undines are the beings of Water, and are present in all natural waters: rain, streams, rivers and the sea. They prefer water which is moving but can be attracted to still water, so long as it is cold, as they need conditions which are cold and wet. To invoke them, you will need to collect a bucket full of water from a natural source, and to use it within 24 hrs before it loses its 'life'. Use incense of sandalwood or cedar wood. After your invocation, gently place your hand deep into the water and, if you are fortunate, you will feel the Undines moving in the water around your fingers.

Gnomes, the beings of Earth, are found in all forms of earth. They are the beings which gave rise to the myths of Gnomes in fairy stories, but unlike any description you will have come across before. They are so slow moving that they are almost beyond the reach of

elements: the cornerstones of magic

our senses. Probably the best way to come into contact with them is by lying full length on the earth and feeling for their presence with your mind. Place a few drops of musk or patchouli oil onto the ground to encourage them to make themselves known. If you intend to work indoors, then immerse your hands into a large bowl or tray of freshly gathered earth. Gnomes prefer conditions which are cold and dry and are often easier to detect when the earth is cool; winter or early morning.

ABOUT RITUALS

Do not be put off by the term Ritual. A Ritual is simply a series of Rites, or actions, brought together to make a whole. The central part of a Craft Ritual is usually a spell or spells. Rituals are not necessarily performed by groups of people; they are often performed by Solitary Witches. The usual complete format of a Ritual is as follows:

Prepare the area – that is clearing a space large enough for what you intend to do. If you are on your own and do not need a lot of equipment you will only need enough space to stand, kneel or sit, without falling over things!

Set the Altar – which simply means gathering together in one place everything you will need. Again, if you are on your own you may only need space for a candle, or some incense. Of course, occasionally you may need space for more. At times, an 'Altar' may even be a designated area on the ground or the floor. It is simply a question of having somewhere where everything is together, making it easier to avoid losing, or tripping over things.

Invoke the Elements – which, as you have practised above, becomes quicker and easier the more experience you have.

the real witches' craft

Invite the Goddess and the God – we will work on this later in the book, but for now I will introduce a very simple form of this.

Cast the Circle – if the purpose of the Ritual involves raising energy and directing it to make a spell work, then a proper Circle is needed, but as this Ritual is intended for personal development you do not yet need a formal Circle.

Raising the energy for a spell – which I will go into in more detail later.

Performing the spell or other purpose.

Grounding or earthing – which is sometimes performed by the Rite of Wine and Cakes and at others is simply having something to eat and drink after tidying up.

Dismissing the Quarters – as you have read above.

Thanking the Goddess and the God.

Taking down the Circle – only if it was required.

Tidying up – which is simply putting things away.

This may all seem quite complex, but is in fact very straightforward. Whilst in a Coven the process may be quite formal, a person on their own can do most of this in their mind using the skills developed in this book. As this is the first Ritual in this book I am going to use the slightly more formal way of calling the Elements, but if you are practised you can do this in your mind.

elements: the cornerstones of magic

THE ELEMENTAL RITUAL

First, select which of the four Elemental forms you would like to experience. Then get, or create, the medium which they inhabit; incense for Sylphs, flame for Salamanders, water for Undines and earth for Gnomes. If you wish you can also light incense of the scent they prefer and a candle of the appropriate colour; yellow for Sylphs, red for Salamanders, blue for Undines or green for Gnomes. Please ensure that any candles and incense are in secure fire-proof holders and cannot set anything alight. Have to hand your magical journal or Book of Shadows. You will also need some matches. Place these together on the surface you have designated as your Altar area. Spend a little time reviewing your experiences with this particular Element and its associations, and in considering what you hope to achieve with your Ritual. Also consider your personal state of mind: are you personally in balance, and if not where does the imbalance lie? Address this using the techniques above.

Select a time when you are not likely to be disturbed or interrupted. Turn off the ringer on the phone, or put it out of hearing. Ensure pets are settled, and so on. When you are sure you are ready to begin, start by creating the Sacred Space as mentioned earlier.

Invoke the Elements:

Standing in the East, and facing that direction, call on the Element of Air saying:

'I call upon the Element of Air, to join with me here in this Circle.'

When you can actually feel the presence of Air, say:

'Blessed Be.'

the real witches' craft

Then call Fire in the South, Water in the West, and Earth in the North.

Next invite the Goddess and the God:

Still facing the North, close your eyes, visualize the Goddess and the God and say:

'Gracious Goddess, Mighty God, I call upon you to guide me, guard me and protect me in these my Rites. Blessed Be.'

Then cast the Circle:

Lastly, move to the North-East of the Circle and with the forefinger of your strong hand draw a circle in the air around the outer boundary of the Circle. As you do so, visualize an electric blue light creating a circle which becomes a sphere containing the whole circle, and say:

'I do cast this Circle as a place of containment and protection. A place between the worlds and a time outside of time.'

Make sure that you overlap the start and finish points of the circle and then say:

'Blessed Be.'

Remember to move Deosil at all times.

Light the incense and candle if you choose to have them. Sit or kneel before the Elemental's medium and gaze into it. Focus your mind on the Element and invite the appropriate Elemental to come to it, by reciting three times the appropriate invitation from the ones below:

elements: the cornerstones of magic

'Gracious Sylphs, beings of the Air, I call upon you. I freely give this offering of incense, that, if it please you, you will come forth and let me know of your presence. Blessed Be.'

'Mighty Salamanders, beings of the flame, I call upon you. I freely give this offering of fire, that, if it please you, you will come forth and let me know of your presence. Blessed Be.'

'Elegant Undines, beings of the Water, I call upon you. I freely give this offering of natural water, that, if it please you, you will come forth and let me know of your presence. Blessed Be.'

'Noble Gnomes, beings of the Earth, I call upon you. I freely give this offering of living earth, that, if it please you, you will come forth and let me know of your presence. Blessed Be.'

Continue to look at and focus on the Element in question. With your mind, consider all its aspects – what it is like at its gentlest and fiercest, the effects it has on the land, plants, and in your life. Include all its associations or correspondences. Recall all of your experiences of working with it. Continue doing this until you perceive an Elemental is present. When this happens, try to clear your mind of all conscious thoughts and simply focus on the Elemental. Try not to force your thoughts, but rather relax and allow your senses to 'observe'. You may find thoughts, sensations or even images coming to you; do not attempt to analyse these at the time, but try to remember them for later. When the Elemental departs, or you can no longer hold your attention, thank them. You should give your thanks whether you thought they were there or not, as they may be present without showing themselves.

'Gracious Sylphs, beings of the Air, I thank you. May you depart in peace to your realm of the skies and the winds. Blessed Be.'

the real witches' craft

'Mighty Salamanders, beings of the Fire, I thank you. May you depart in peace to your realm of Sun and flame. Blessed Be.'

'Elegant Undines, beings of the Water, I thank you. May you depart in peace to your realm of water and the oceans. Blessed Be.'

'Noble Gnomes, beings of the Earth, I thank you. May you depart in peace to your realm of the rocks and the soil. Blessed Be.'

Before removing the Sacred Space make notes on any thoughts, feelings or impressions you felt. Also include your thoughts on them.

Dismiss the Elements:

Standing in the East, and facing that direction, call on the Element of Air, saying:

'I give thanks to the Element of Air, for joining with me here in the Circle. Hale and farewell. Blessed Be.'

Repeat in the South for Fire, West for Water and North for Earth.

Next thank the Goddess and the God:

Still facing the North, close your eyes, and say:

'I give thanks to the Goddess and the God for being present here with me in these my Rites. Hale and farewell. Blessed Be.'

Then remove the Circle:

Move to the North-East of the Circle and with the forefinger of your strong hand draw a circle in the air around the outer boundary of the Circle. This time visualize the electric blue sphere fading and dissipating, and say:

'I remove this Circle and return this place as it was before.'

Make sure that you overlap the start and finish points of the Circle and then say:

'Blessed Be.'

Wait a further five minutes before extinguishing incense or flame, or before disposing of water or earth, so that the Elemental(s) may leave at their own pace. Water or earth should be returned to the land sensitively, not just dumped. During this time it is a good idea to have something to eat and drink, even if it is only a glass of water and a biscuit, to ground yourself. Magical work of any kind brings that part of you which operates on the psychic plane to the fore, and you need to redress this before returning to dealing with the material realm. After all, you wouldn't want to be driving on the same road as someone who was partly in a trance!

When you feel you would like to repeat this Ritual for the other Elementals, remember to only try to contact one form in any one Ritual, and one Ritual in any one day. Remember, practice of the Craft should enhance your life, not take it over.

As I mentioned earlier, knowledge of the Elements is essential to the practice of the Craft and to making spells and magic work. Furthermore, the invocation of the Elements when making the Sacred Space is a key part of this, for it draws their energies from both within and without. With a little practice you will not need to do this in as formal a way as here, as you will be able to invoke and banish using visualization only. But it is a good idea to be able to use either technique. Having said that, there is no reason why you should need to speak the above invocations out loud, you can say the words in your head if you prefer.

THE ELEMENTS AND THE WEATHER

Whilst the Elements we refer to are not the same as the weather, they are associated with each other in many people's minds. Sometimes the term 'the Elements' is used to mean or describe the weather. Certainly, one of the expected, and very useful, skills of the Witch is the ability to predict and even to change weather conditions. From the perspective of the Craft it is not necessary to do either of these on a large scale; we are usually only interested in what affects a small local area and for a short period. It is one thing to ensure you have a dry period for an outdoor event, but we do not want to intervene in the weather to the extent that we upset nature's own balance. Like many other forms of magic, it is also as well to be aware that changes are possible, but not miracles. Whilst you may be able to achieve a warmish day in winter, there is no point in seeking a heatwave!

The first step towards working with the weather lies in understanding it. To do this it is helpful to observe it carefully. Not just whether it is raining or not, but by looking at the direction and strength of the wind, and the shapes of the clouds. Use your other senses too; quite often you will find that there is a smell similar to moist earth just before rain comes, or that the air tastes different before snow, and so on. Personally, I also find that my nose becomes very cold when rain is on the way! Look, too, at other indicators: quite often animals and small children behave in different ways before a change of weather. If you live in the country you will probably be aware that livestock tend to lie down before rain, and huddle together when it is going to get

elements: the cornerstones of magic

colder. Certainly, children become more excitable and restless before the wind picks up, as any observant parent or teacher can tell you. Practise looking at the sky and the signs regularly and you may save yourself getting caught out by sudden changes in weather.

Once you are attuned to the weather and the seasons then you can consider working magic to make change when you truly need to.

Weather Workings

Most people are familiar with the children's chant *'Rain, rain, go away, come again another day.'* Or its variant, *'Rain, rain, go away, come again by night not day.'* Both of these can be worked as spells, so long as they are performed with balance, focus and intent.

To perform them effectively, as with all spells, invoke the Elements and call upon the Goddess and the God. Say either of the spells three times, whilst actually being outdoors in the rain. Remember to dismiss the Elements and thank the Goddess and the God afterwards, and expect results to be soon but not necessarily immediate.

A similar spell goes, *'The clouds are sheep, the wind their shepherd. Shepherd, take your sheep away.'* This is intended to remove both clouds and rain.

To raise a wind, perhaps to dry washing, stand with your back to whatever air movement there is, and blow three times whilst focusing on a *gentle* increase in wind.

'Delayed magic' can also be worked. It used to be common, but is now much less so, for sailors to 'buy the wind' from a Witch. The Witch would tie three knots in a cord, which the sailor could untie at need. The first is for a breeze, the second for a wind and the third for a strong wind. In this case, the Witch would have used magic to visualize and tie each form of wind into the cord, so that it could be later released.

Every Coven I know of has its own weather worker, usually the person who shows most natural skill at this kind of magic. It is their task to try to ensure that conditions are as good as possible when outdoor rituals are intended. This form of 'in advance' magic is worked keeping in mind the seasonal norm, for instance, if it is winter then the spell is worked to make the Ritual site a little warmer and drier than might be expected. The worker will visit the site in good weather, then when they need to work the magic they will use all their experiences of that visit to create a spell which comes as close as possible to the preferred weather. This is not to say that Witches avoid the cold or wet, for we are nature based, but some places can be unsafe if it is particularly inclement. Likewise, there are some events which can be nearly intolerable if it is too hot; I have tried to do a dance and chant workshop in brilliant sunshine, but I'd rather not!

However, knowledge and understanding of the Elements is simply the first step towards working effective magic, so I'd like to move on to some of the other steps.

Chapter Two

CREATING THE POWER
TO MAKE MAGIC

Magic doesn't just happen because you say the 'right' words or go through the 'right' movements. Nor is it cookery; simply putting the 'ingredients' together to get a result. There is more to the practice of effective magic than simply assembling the 'right' tools, equipment, candles and crystals and saying the 'right' words. For spells and magic to work they have to have energy, which is also needed to focus and send the magic to its intended destination. Much of this energy comes from the person working the magic, which is why magical working is usually quite tiring. Indeed, if you are not tired after working magic, then you are probably not putting enough of yourself into it.

The energy used in magical working comes from outside as well as from within. It is in part the energy of the Elements, which we discussed in the first chapter. But it is also that of the Goddess and the God who we call upon when we create the Sacred Space. But most of all, it is our own personal energy which can be harnessed and directed. This is often referred to as magical power, and the techniques to access it are called raising power. However, it is important to realize that we are not talking about power, or control, over others, but control of ourselves to create power for use in magical working.

We all have magical power within us, but it is usually dormant until we learn to access it. For many people it is also suppressed in our younger years, as demonstrating any 'unusual' ability has been, for a long time, considered not 'nice'. It is thought by some that it is the combination of this suppression and the hormonal changes of adolescence which gives rise to poltergeist activity. For some people, their first experience of magical power can be when they find themselves in extreme circumstances, much in the same way that some people exhibit 'superhuman' strength when a loved one is endangered. However, this is not an effective way of dealing with the day-to-day magic which we want to practise. Moreover, it is usually harder to maintain the focus and control needed when in the grip of extreme emotion. So we need to learn how to harness this energy when we wish.

WAYS OF RAISING ENERGY

Whilst magical power is inherent in everyone, some people find it easier to harness than others. Because of this there are a number of techniques which are often recommended. Since the time of Gerald Gardner these have sometimes been grouped together and called the Eight-fold Path, although that actually encompasses more than eight different methods. Some of these are more appropriate for achieving a state of altered consciousness than for actually raising energy for magical working. Here I will give the Eight-fold Path as it is usually depicted, but will discuss its components separately. All of them are intended to create a state of altered consciousness, but it is important that this is controlled, otherwise the practitioner will not be able to focus and control the power.

creating the power to make magic

1 Meditation or concentration

In meditation, the mind is focused solely on a single objective, to the exclusion of all other thoughts. For some people this comes very easily, for others it can take months of regular practice to be able to achieve it. Unless you have a very strongly developed will, or in exceptional cases a very strong feeling attached to your magic, then meditation and concentration are rarely enough to raise power for magical work. However, as meditation and visualization are both crucial to the working of effective magic, and not just to raise power, chapters four and five deal with them in some detail.

2 Chants, spells, calls and invocations

Chants are one of the most popular ways of raising power in the Craft today. They are used in groups and by individuals alike. Sometimes they are used on their own, at other times they may be combined with dance and/or music. There are a great number of chants in common use, many of which you can learn at conferences and the like, or which appear on CDs, including my own. Alternatively, you can create your own.

'Spells' is used here in a slightly confusing way as it refers not to pieces of magic, as in 'a candle spell', but to verses, whether rhyming or not, which are used in a spell as in the verses for weather magic in the preceding chapter. Again, there are many spells available today in books and the like, or you can write your own. It is usually the repetition of the verse which makes it take effect as it is actually a method of focusing the mind on the desired magic.

Calls are usually wordless cries which are sometimes combined with dancing. They are a common feature of ritual dances in many non-western societies, especially those which have strong traditions of inducing states of altered consciousness.

Invocation is the act of calling upon a deity or spirit in such a way that their presence and energy come to the person invoking them. Drawing down the Moon is a powerful invocation which is covered in detail towards the end of this chapter.

3 Trance and astral projection

Very few people are capable of entering a trance state whilst still maintaining the focus necessary to perform effective magic.

Astral projection is a form of trance in which you send your astral body, or spirit, out of your physical form and travel elsewhere. Whilst some people find this easy, there are also those who never master the technique. Should you be one of the fortunate few who find it easy to astrally project, it is important that you do so safely. You need to ensure that both your astral and physical forms are safe at all times, and take care that you know how to return at any time. Certainly, it is not something which is easy to learn through reading, and you may need to find an experienced mentor to assist you. Personally, I feel that neither trance nor astral projection are going to be successful ways of raising power for the vast majority of people, although working on the astral is a different matter.

4 Incense, wine and other aids to release the spirit

The practice of burning herbs and other substances has long been used to create a state of altered consciousness. Indeed, other forms of fragrance can also be used, as they are in aromatherapy. There are many blends of incense around or you can make up your own. If you choose to do the latter it is as well to test anything you create before you actually intend to use it, as you do not want to fill your home with an evil-smelling fog, even if it is effective!

creating the power to make magic

Again, alcohol has been used for thousands of years, but there is a very fine line between the amount which will help to release the spirit and the amount which can interfere with, rather than enhance, magical working.

No responsible person would advise the use of any kind of drugs, whether legal or otherwise, to achieve a state of altered consciousness. Furthermore, it has been found that those who do use them in this way subsequently have enormous difficulty in being able to work without them. Having said that, there are many household herbs which can be made into teas which can help with accessing the subconscious mind, and which are very effective in psychic readings rather than in power raising.

5 Dancing

Again, dancing has a very long history as a way of achieving an altered state of mind. In group workings the circle dance is a very effective way of raising power, and the solitary Witch can dance magic into working. The most effective dances all include moving in a circular motion. To gain a brief taste for this, try spinning on the spot for just a minute: when you stop you should detect a change in your perceptions.

6 Blood control and use of the cords

Using cords to bind a person with the intention of reducing the flow of blood to achieve a state of altered consciousness is something which I do not recommend. Whilst it is possible for a skilled person to tie another in such a way as to achieve this, for the Solitary it is fraught with hideous potentialities, including the possibility of causing brain damage or even death. However, there are safer ways of controlling the flow of blood, such as those used in yoga to slow the heart rate.

7 The scourge

Regular rhythmic use of the scourge can induce a trance-like state, but it is not something that very many people feel comfortable with. Furthermore, it is virtually impossible to achieve on your own.

8 The Great Rite

The Great Rite is a part of Ritual which is usually carried out by a working partnership of Witches. The Rite involves a Priest and Priestess invoking the Goddess and the God into one another and then celebrating their union. It can take place symbolically; in which case the union will be performed with Chalice and Athame in a similar way to the Rite of Wine and Cakes; in token, where the Priest will overlay the Priestess but not penetrate her; or actual, in which the rite is consummated. Note that the Rite of Wine and Cakes, however, has neither the same intent nor effect as the Great Rite; they just appear similar.

Outside of the Eight-fold Path, there are other ways of raising energy: limited fasting; drumming and clapping and other forms of music; working with strong feelings and emotions; giving energy form; grounding; and certain Rituals, such as Drawing down the Moon and the Charge of the Goddess.

FASTING

One method of enhancing your ability to raise power and to work magic which is not included in the Eight-fold Path is to limit the food and drink you put into your body, or partial fasting. Note that this is not the same as starving yourself! For the first 18 hours of the 24-hour period prior to your magical working you limit your food intake to fresh fruit only, taking no food at all for the final six hours before the working. For the whole of this

24-hour period you may drink as much water or plain herbal tea as you wish. Obviously, you should not do this if you have any kind of illness or have a hectic schedule, nor should you do this more than once a month. This cleansing regime will enhance your ability to raise power, and to focus and control it.

MUSIC

Another aid to raising power which is not actually mentioned in the Eight-fold Path is the use of music, although it is perhaps implied in the sections on chant, dance and calls. A timeless technique, music of one kind or another has a long history of being used to enhance magical working. This is especially true of drumming and other forms of percussion, including clapping, and of singing. You only have to go to a well-attended performance of vibrant music to be able to see the way that the atmosphere becomes charged. Performers will tell you that they can feel the energy of the audience rising when their music is appreciated, and that they in turn can use that energy to enhance their performance. Many Witches use music to enhance their working, either creating it themselves or sometimes using pre-recorded pieces. It is worth noting, though, that as many electronic items malfunction when taken into the Circle, the actual machinery is best situated outside of the Circle.

Of all the above techniques, probably the most successful for actually raising power are the use of music, chants and dance, whilst limited fasting will enhance any kind of magical working.

the real witches' craft

PRACTICAL WORK 1

Experiment with several different kinds of recorded music to see which you find raises your energy levels. You might also like to try different volume levels (although try not to offend those you live with or near to!) and different levels of bass and treble. Most people find that repetitive music with a definite base beat works best, and often that instrumental is better than that with vocals, although there are some chants tapes and CDs where the vocals complement the Craft rather than distract the attention. You might also like to listen to regional, traditional and ethnic pieces, as these often have their roots in Goddess worship. If you can find pieces which build in pace and volume you may also find that these are more effective too. When you have found a few pieces of music then try playing them within the cast Circle to see which still feel strong.

Take this a step further by clapping along to the rhythm, starting by a single clap to the beat and increasing this to two, three or four claps per beat. The idea is to increase the energy input progressively so that the power builds. If you have a drum you could also experiment using this. In most cases it is better to drum with the hands rather than using any kind of stick as the idea is to raise power, not to be as loud as you can.

As with many of the exercises in this book, don't expect instant results. Most things related to the Craft take time to learn and develop the necessary skills. Remember to write up your thoughts and feelings.

creating the power to make magic

PRACTICAL WORK 2

Once you have found some music which appeals to you, try expressing yourself through dancing to it. Incorporate circular and spinning movements in your dance. Practise until you find a dance which you can feel building energy. Initially, do this without casting a Circle; that way, although you will detect the rising energy it will be able to dissipate quickly, rather than leaving you with unfocused power.

Don't worry if you feel self-conscious at first; most of us do, although you may find it easier if you can ensure that you will not be seen by others! When you feel ready, try this in the Circle at a time when you have a simple spell to perform and see if you can detect the difference in your magical power.

PRACTICAL WORK 3

Search out some Pagan and Wiccan chants; the Witchcraft Museum at Boscastle produces a CD and my own Coven has also released one of their own. Look for chants which are simple to learn, and repetitive. Learn a couple of these and practise them with, and without, drumming or clapping. Start slowly and gradually increase the pace until you are chanting as fast as you can. The advantage of producing your own music is that you can vary the pace to build the energy you develop.

In the Craft we tend to use a sequence of three or four chants, each repeated several times, and often ending with a repeat of the first. To give you some idea of this, the following is a sequence we might use, each of the chants being repeated four times before moving on to the next:

'Isis, Astarte, Diana, Hecate, Demeter, Kali, Inanna.'

'Lady of the Moon, Lady of the Moon. Come to us, be with us, Lady of the Moon.'

'Power of the music, Power of the song, Power of the magic, Pass the magic on.'

'Isis, Astarte, Diana, Hecate, Demeter, Kali, Inanna.'

creating the power to make magic

If you have worked through the above exercises you will know how it feels when energy has been raised and should also be aware of the effect it can have on your magic.

WORKING WITH EMOTIONS

There are also ways of raising energy which do not require physical activity, but these are, for most people, much harder to achieve and control. One of these techniques is evoking and focusing very strong feelings. The problem with this is, as mentioned above, that it is quite difficult to focus and direct energies when we are personally involved. However, it is worth working on this, as for some people it can be very effective.

PRACTICAL WORK 4

Think back to an occasion when you were in the grip of very strong feelings. It is important that you choose an occasion sufficiently in the past for you to be able to distance yourself from the feeling, whilst at the same time being able to revisit it.

Think through all the circumstances of that occasion until you can actually 'feel' the emotion in question. While you are doing this, try to separate the emotion from the energy that is building within you. This is not easy and you may need to experiment with several memories and feelings. For some people, anger is often the easiest to work with as, whilst we can recall it, it is easier to distance ourselves from the actual emotion. But another feeling which can be accessed is fear: if you think back to a really scary moment in a film, you can often recall the energy-surge you felt, whilst being unaffected by the fear, which you now know to have been generated by the skills of the movie makers.

Once you have identified the feeling of energy rising within you, see if you can take hold of that and bring it into being by thought alone. For most people this will need a lot of practice, but if you persevere you will be able to summon energy at will.

As you practise techniques for raising energy you will soon learn which are most effective for you. You will also find that you can easily tell the difference between effective energy raising and the occasions when it does not come readily. You can use this knowledge to help you to determine when you are in a position to work effective magic. For we all have times when it is better not to try to work our spells. This may be because we are tired or ill. But it can also be because our elements are unbalanced, so if you feel sure that you are well and sufficiently rested you might try to revisit some of the exercises from the preceding chapter before trying again. Of course, there will also be some occasions when magic does not work for reasons which are not easy to identify; in this case it is better to put it aside and perhaps try again the following day.

Having the ability to raise energy is not enough on its own; we need to contain it, which is why we cast the Circle before starting our magic. The Circle has two functions: one is to contain the energy we have raised, otherwise it would simply dissipate rather than building up. The second function is that of protection; for once we open up our inner mind to allow the release of energy, we also open ourselves to energy from outside, and not all energies may be positive. The negative thoughts and feelings of those around us can also influence us and the magic we work, and the Circle protects us from these. Another way we can protect both ourselves and our magic, as well as build the maximum amount of energy, is by keeping silent about our magic. When we tell others about our magical intentions, there is firstly the possibility that someone may find out who could disapprove of the spell. This person may actively, or subconsciously, send negative energy in our direction, which could influence either us or the spell itself. This is why, when you work magic with others, everyone has to agree with the nature of the magic, for even passive disapproval will influence it. Not only that, but the more we discuss our intention, the more we reduce the actual energy we can put into it. Think of it this way: when you are upset by someone or something, you tell others and gradually the telling reduces your strong feelings. Likewise in magic, the more you talk about your intention, the more you dissipate the energy you could have directed towards it.

the real witches' craft

GIVING FORM TO ENERGY

For many Witches it is not enough simply to think about raising energy, it helps to give that energy a form. One of these forms is called the Cone of Power. In this, the energy is raised in a circular manner into an upward-pointed cone, which rises above the centre of the Circle. The energy is built up, layer by layer, using the base of the Circle as its starting point, and rising high above. It is usually visualized as a white, or electric-blue light, which can be focused into a powerful beam. Once the Cone comes to a point, and it is felt that no more energy can be added, it is released towards its intended destination. The Cone of Power can also be used as a sort of beacon, especially in magic which is intended to draw something or someone towards you, as when seeking a teacher or mentor in the Craft, or when looking for a Coven.

Another form is that of the Earth Dragon. This is most usually used in earth healing magics. This huge dragon is visualized as being coiled up within the planet. It can help to visualize the Earth as seen from space, and it is woken by the raising of energy, before being directed towards the needs of the planet or nature.

creating the power to make magic

PRACTICAL WORK 5

Find a picture or photograph of the Earth as seen from space; if you can find a selection of views you may find it helpful. Next find an image of a dragon; one which looks powerful, but is also attractive to you. If you can, make the dragon picture very nearly as large as the Earth image. Then superimpose the dragon over the image of the Earth. Place this composite picture somewhere you can see it and spend a few minutes each day contemplating it. As you do so, try to visualize the dragon actually blending into the planet.

Once you can do this, then move on to visualizing the dragon uncoiling from the Earth and flying, deosil, around the planet. Practise these visualizations, without trying to work any magic with them, until you feel that you can really see the dragon in your mind's eye. At this point you may find that the dragon in your mind is not the same as the one in the picture, but this is quite usual. Many of us find that the visualized Earth Dragon becomes quite 'real' to us with practice, and takes on a life of its own. As with other exercises, make a point of noting down your thoughts and feelings after each session, and this way you should be able to see your progress.

In addition to raising energy we also need to direct it effectively, which we do by focusing on the object of the magic, not only at the point of releasing the energy, but also whilst we are raising it. For this we use visualization and various magical tools and aids, such as images and candles, etc. Both tools and visualization will be covered in detail later in this book.

GROUNDING AND EARTHING

After every act of magic, spell, rite or ritual we should also 'ground' or 'earth' ourselves. Working magic of any kind invariably means accessing a state of altered consciousness and we need to ensure that we return fully to the 'here and now'. Otherwise, you may find that you do not function as well in your daily life as you normally do – it can be quite dangerous say crossing the road, or driving a car, to be even partially on an ethereal plane! Also, when we have raised power for an act of magic, we may not have fully discharged this energy, and this can interfere with daily functioning. It is just as important to ground yourself after meditation, or even a period of intense concentration which may not be associated with Craft.

There are several ways of grounding or earthing ourselves:

Probably the simplest is to have a warm or sweet drink and something to eat. This not only goes some way towards replenishing the energy you have put in, but also gets the body's physical systems working on a basic level.

If you are outside, earthing can be achieved by placing the hands and bare feet onto the land itself and allowing excess energy to pass into the land.

Another technique is to vigorously rub your arms and legs.

In all cases you should easily recognize the difference in feeling between your magical self and the normal 'you'.

creating the power to make magic

PRACTICAL WORK 6

Choose a time when you are certain you will not be disturbed, or required to perform any daily activity for at least an hour. Before you start, make a hot or sweet drink and a light snack. Place these somewhere safe in the room you are working in. Also have to hand a simple activity unrelated to the Craft, possibly the TV listings page to read or a simple manual puzzle. Avoid anything which is related to fire, electrical equipment, or is otherwise likely to be risky if you cannot focus your full attention on it!

Cast the Circle in your usual way and raise energy, using whichever of the techniques you find most effective. However, instead of working a spell, just move straight on to removing the Circle. Now attempt your activity. Notice how you feel and how easy or difficult you find it to concentrate on your task.

Next, rub your arms and legs vigorously as well as having your drink and snack. Do both because you are performing a fairly extreme experiment; usually you would not raise energy just to 'see how it feels'. Perform your task again and notice the differences between your first and second attempts.

If you are still working on developing your ability to raise energy and don't feel confident that you will be successful, try the following instead: Prepare the food and drink as before, but instead of casting the Circle and raising power, spin around for a full minute before attempting the task. Then earth yourself as described in the previous paragraph and try it again. This is not quite the same, but will give you a rough idea of the need for grounding and earthing. Again make notes on your experiences.

DRAWING DOWN THE MOON

Another way of raising energy is the rite called Drawing Down the Moon, which takes place at the Full Moon. In the modern Craft this has become quite formalized, with a Priest invoking the spirit of the Goddess into a Priestess who then proclaims the Charge of the Goddess to the rest of the Coven. Drawing Down the Moon, when performed successfully, channels the spirit of the Goddess through the Priestess, and the Charge then becomes the words of the Goddess addressed to Her followers. However, this format for Drawing Down the Moon, as given in most 'modern' books on the Craft, implies that the Rite is only for those who work in groups or Covens, but this does not have to be the case. There are techniques for Drawing Down the Moon which can be an effective way of raising energy for the solitary Witch.

For the sake of completeness I have included the group, or Coven, form of Drawing Down the Moon, and also a Full Moon Ritual which can be used by the Solitary Witch.

The Priestess stands with her back to the Altar, preferably facing the Moon. The Priest commences by giving her the Five-fold Kiss. The Priestess now allows her hands to move slightly away from her sides with her palms facing forward. Whilst he continues she should look over his head at the full Moon and focus on allowing the spirit of the Goddess to enter her.

creating the power to make magic

With the forefinger of his strong hand the Priest then touches the Priestess in the sigil of the First Degree: right breast, left breast, womb and right breast, whilst saying:

'I invoke thee and call upon thee Mighty Mother of us all, bringer of all fruitfulness, by seed and root, by stem and bud, by flower and fruit do I invoke thee, to descend upon this the body of thy servant and Priestess.'

He then kneels and, spreading his arms outwards and downwards, says:

'Hail Aradia, from the Amalthean Horn. Pour forth thy store of love. I lowly bend before thee, I adore thee to the end. With loving sacrifice thy shrine adorn. Thy foot is to my lip.'

He kisses her feet and continues:

'My prayer, upon the rising incense upborne. Then spend thine ancient love O Mighty One, descend to aid me, for without thee I am forlorn.'

The Priest then rises and faces the group and says:

'Listen to the words of the Great Mother, she who, of old, was also called among men Artemis, Astarte, Dione, Melusine, Aphrodite, Ceridwyn, Dana, Arianrhod, Isis, Bride and many other names.'

He then steps to the side and the Priestess, facing the group, raises her arms and delivers the Charge.

the real witches' craft

There are two key components to this Rite. The first is the ability of an experienced Priest to invoke the Goddess, which can help even the least experienced Priestess to become the vessel of the Goddess. However, the second component, the ability of the Priestess to open her mind to the Goddess, will enhance the Rite, or can help an inexperienced Priest to learn the technique. Obviously, for a Solitary Witch, the latter is essential, as she will be on her own.

creating the power to make magic

PRACTICAL WORK 7
— LUNAR DIARY

Every night for a full lunar month (29 days) take the time to look at the Moon. You may need to provide yourself with a diary or calendar which also indicates the time of Moonrise in your part of the world. It is best if you can actually go outside, or at least open the window, but if this really is impossible, then look through the glass. Notice the phase of the Moon; for example, new, first quarter, full, third quarter, or dark, where no Moon is visible. Also take note of whether the Moon is waxing (increasing in size), or waning (decreasing). Even if the sky is clouded over, you should be able to work out its phase. As you do so, consider which aspect of the Goddess this reflects. Keep a record of the Moon; its size, rising time, and position in the sky. If you are able to get outside, notice where the Moonlight actually falls, as the Moon also casts shadows. Alongside these, note how you feel physically, emotionally and spiritually, both in your daily life and whilst performing the exercise. You may like to continue this diary even when you have worked through this chapter, as you will also find it helpful for work later in this book.

SOLITARY DRAWING DOWN THE MOON

As with all Rituals, ensure that you have prepared yourself and everything you will need, including some means of grounding yourself afterwards.

On the night of the full Moon, position yourself so that you can kneel upright, rather than back on your heels, facing the Moon, in its light. Whilst standing, create the Sacred Space in your usual way.

Then kneel in the moonlight, and raise your arms to each side of your head, so that they curve gently upwards. Close your eyes and take several deep breaths to centre yourself. Open your eyes and gaze at the Moon, or just above it as this is better for the eyes. Whilst you do so, focus your mind on the Mother Goddess. You may also like to consider chanting, *'Lady of the Moon, Lady of the Moon. Come to us, be with us, Lady of the Moon,'* several times, either aloud, or under your breath. Consider all that she does for you and for the land. Visualize Her energy being carried in the Moonlight, washing over and entering you. When you are sure you can feel her energy within you, read aloud the Charge of the Goddess (below) quietly to yourself, then spend a few moments in meditation. If you have an act of magic you wish to perform at this Esbat, do so now.

When you are ready, remove the Sacred Space in the usual way and ground yourself before going on to tidy up and write up your notes.

Many Witches find that Drawing Down the Moon is a very empowering Ritual, and that it has energizing effects which last well beyond the night it was performed.

creating the power to make magic

THE CHARGE OF THE GODDESS

The Charge may be derived from Doreen Valiente's Charge of the Goddess, as is the version given below. But it may also be written by the High Priestess, or the Priestess may speak the words which come to her at the time. It is usually recommended that Priestesses memorize the Charge, even though when the time comes in the ritual they may find that other words will come to them.

'Whenever ye have need of any thing, once in the month, and better it be if the Moon is full, then shall ye gather in some secret place and worship the spirit of me, who art Queen of all Witcheries. There shall ye assemble, ye who would fain learn all sorcery, yet have not won its deepest secrets, to these I shall teach things as yet unknown. And ye shall be free from slavery, and as a sign that ye be really free, ye shall be naked in your Rites. And ye shall dance, sing, feast, make music and love, all in my praise. For mine is the ecstasy of the spirit, and mine is also joy on earth, for my lore is love unto all things. Keep pure your highest ideals, strive ever towards them, let naught stop you, nor turn you aside. For mine is the secret door which opens on to the land of youth, and mine is the cup of the wine of life, and the Cauldron of Cerridwen, which is the Holy Grail of immortality.

'For I am the gracious Goddess, who gives the gift of the joy of life unto the hearts of man. Upon earth I give knowledge of the spirit eternal, and beyond death, I give peace and freedom, and reunion with those who have gone before. Nor do I demand sacrifice, for behold I am the gracious Mother of all living, and my love is poured out upon the earth. I who am the beauty of the green earth, and the white Moon amongst the stars, and the mystery of the waters, and the desire of the heart of man, call unto thy soul; arise and come unto me. For I am the soul of

nature, who gives life to the universe. From me all things proceed, and unto me all things must return; and before my face, beloved of Gods and of men, let thine innermost self be enfolded in the rapture of the infinite. Let my worship be within the heart that rejoiceth; for behold, all acts of love and pleasure are my rituals. And therefore let there be beauty and strength, power and compassion, honour and humility, mirth and reverence within you. And thou who thinkest to seek for me, know that thy seeking and yearning shall avail ye not, unless thou knowest the mystery; that if that which thou seekest, thou findest not within thee, then thou shalt never find it without. For behold, I have been with thee from the beginning, and I am that which is attained at the end of all desire.'

DRAWING DOWN THE SUN

Whilst there is no reason that a Priest should not be able to channel the energy of the Goddess for his magic, there is a complementary Ritual known as Drawing Down the Sun. This is performed in much the same way, although it is essential that neither Priest nor Priestess looks at the Sun itself, as this can so easily damage the eyesight. In many cases a golden, but not reflective, disc or other solar symbol is placed so that the sunlight falls onto it and the Priest uses this as the focus of his concentration. Drawing Down the Sun is usually performed when the Sun is at its zenith and is therefore a daytime ritual. Whilst Drawing Down the Moon is often performed every month, Drawing Down the Sun takes place far less often, usually only at the Summer and Winter Solstices, as the Craft is a Lunar based belief system and it is the Goddess to whom we primarily look for the source of our magics. The God is her Consort and Her partner through the Wheel of the Year, and the changing of the seasons.

creating the power to make magic

There is no well-known equivalent Charge of the God, although many have written their own, but some use a version of the Song of Amergin:

'I am the Wind of the Sea.
I am the Wave of the Sea.
I am the Sound of the Sea.
I am the Stag of Seven Tines.
I am the Hawk upon the Cliff.
I am the Ray of the Sun.
I am the Fairest among Flowers.
I am the Savage Boar in Valour.
I am the Salmon in the Pool.
I am the Lake upon the Plain.
I am the Hill of Poetry.
I am the Spear Point in the Battle.
I am the God who kindles the Fire Within.
Who, but I, can make known the Secrets of the Unhewn Dolman?
Who, but I, can make known the Ages of the Moon?
Who, but I, can show the Secrets of the Resting Sun?'

At one time the Song of Amergin was thought to be a Christian text, but it can actually be traced back as far as 600BC, and may well be far older. More recently it has been considered to be a Druid verse, but there is little, if any, evidence that it should be considered exclusive to them.

ENERGY SPELLS

Whilst we raise energy for each spell or piece of magic we work, there are some magics which are centred on specific forms of power raising.

the real witches' craft

Building the Cone of Power to draw something to you

One of the frequently asked questions of the Craft is, 'How do I find a Coven, or a teacher or mentor, or a magical co-worker?' The first step is to determine what you actually need, not in terms of a specific person or group, but in terms of your requirements.

To expand: if you are seeking a Coven, how often will you be able to attend? Sabbats, Esbats, and new Moons mean 33 dates per year, almost certainly mostly evenings. Consider how far you are prepared to travel, bearing in mind that many meetings may finish after public transport stops running. Are you able and willing to work outside, or might adverse weather have an effect on your health? Are you looking for a formal structure, with regular training sessions, or one where you are required to make a greater effort to drive your own learning.

Alternatively, if you are looking for a mentor or partner, would you feel happier, at least at first, being with someone of your own sex. Would you prefer someone who you can meet regularly or would you be happy with letters and/or emails? Consider which form of the Craft attracts you: hedgewitch, Gardnerian, Alexandrian or another path.

When you have a clear idea of what you are seeking, prepare your area and create your Sacred Space in the usual way. In the centre of your Circle place a single, unlit white candle in a safe holder. Raise energy in your preferred manner, but as you do so visualize a circle of white light rising from the edges of the Circle. Build it up until it becomes a cone rising high above you. As you are doing this, focus on the specifics you decided you are seeking. Visualize the cone becoming a beacon in the skies which will draw to you what you seek. Once it is at its peak, release its base from the Circle, leaving

creating the power to make magic

the beacon to remain above, much like a spotlight pointed into the sky. Now light the candle and keep it by you until it has burnt all the way down. Whilst it is doing so you can complete your ritual in the normal way, and write up your notes.

A word of caution however: if you cannot maintain your focus on the things that you seek, and find your concentration wandering in any other direction, stop the spell immediately and banish both the Circle and however much of the cone you have built. This is to prevent the cone acting as a beacon for things you do not want to draw to you.

EARTH HEALING WITH THE EARTH DRAGON

For some, Earth healing magic is the primary reason for working as a Witch, and they will work magic for the preservation of endangered species, or the rainforest, or to prevent the death of wildlife on our roads, etc. Virtually all their spells will be directed at the healing of the planet and the life which dwells on it. In this case they will use a number of forms of spell working.

For others, it is a form of magic undertaken at times they consider to be of particular need, for example, when there is an oil spill or other potential ecological disaster. Because this is usually directed at a geographical location, raising the Earth Dragon is especially effective for this is a type of magic.

Prepare by researching the problem as well as you can. Watch and listen to TV and radio coverage, read articles on the internet, until you have a clear mental picture of the problem. Try to be aware of the causes: for example, is a rainforest being cleared to make way for the genuine needs of local people or is it being cleared to further the interests of industry? When you are sure that your magical intention is sound, then you can go on to perform your spell at the next full Moon.

If you feel the need, take the picture(s) you created of the Earth Dragon in exercise five into your working area with you. Create your Circle in the usual way. Raise power by whichever technique you have found most effective. Now focus that energy in visualizing and waking the Dragon. Call upon it until you see it rising out of the planet, with its great wings unfurled and its tail stretching out behind it. Watch until you can see it circle the Earth three times. Now focus your energy towards the region which needs help and, stating the nature of the problem, direct the Dragon towards it. Visualize the Dragon swooping down to that area and entering it, plunging deep into the land. Now visualize its presence driving out the problem and restoring the land and life to health and fruitfulness. When you feel sure that the Dragon's work is done, thank it and give it leave to rest once more. Complete your ritual as usual and write up your notes.

Regrettably, few of us have sufficient energy to achieve Earth healing on our own, but it is certain that when many Witches work this form of magic for the good of the land then things do begin to improve. Many Witches feel that each full Moon Ritual should take the form of three spells: one for the self, one for someone else and one for the land.

creating the power to make magic

Chapter Three

DEVELOPING
THE SENSES

I am often asked how to develop psychic powers or the sixth sense, but very few people really use the standard five to full advantage. When we speak about the senses we mean sight, hearing, smell, taste, and touch. It is through these that we perceive and interact with not only the world, but also those around us. And it is only through learning to use them fully that we can begin to develop our sixth sense.

The sixth sense is the one which allows us to predict events and the actions and reactions of people, and to determine what may happen. But much of this can already be determined by the full use of the other five. One of the traditional roles of the Witch or wise-man or woman is as a person who has spent all their life in a small community, who knows the ways of the people, both as a whole and as individuals. They will also know the land, the plants, the livestock and animals and the way they interact with one another. They will be the ones who know which plants grow where and how their seasonality can be used to predict the weather. They will know much about the interrelationships between different individuals and their families, and will be able to predict how they will behave in various situations. This is not magical, but simply the use of many years of keen observation of people and nature. A more modern form of this is practised by others, for example the parent, or partner, who can tell where something was left, not because they looked for it there, but because their observation of their surroundings and knowledge of their family means they 'know without looking', or the person who can tell when another is listening in on a conversation, even when the listener's back is turned. There are many things in life where we 'know', without knowing how we know, and these are often examples of how we have used our five senses more fully than we realize, perhaps less consciously than we usually do. Think back to one of those occasions when you have 'known' something wasn't quite right, for no obvious reason, and have subsequently been proved correct. But if we work on them, we can develop our senses far more fully and from that, begin to develop our sixth sense too.

As a species we actually use our senses in a distinct preferential series. Sight is by far the most important to the human race. Next in importance is sound, followed by touch, smell and taste. There is some debate as to which of the last two is most, or least, important; I would argue that you would be unlikely to voluntarily taste something which smells bad, whereas you might choose to smell something which tastes bad, perfume being a prime example. Moreover, smell is one of the most evocative senses; the scent of newly baked bread, or burning leaves, can transport us back to a whole range of memories.

Having said that, people with sensory disabilities quickly learn to use their other senses to compensate, and in some cases this can be in quite unexpected ways. We are all familiar with the fact that a blind person will use touch, via a cane or stick, to enable them to walk down the street. But a great many blind people can detect colour through their fingertips, which they express as occurring by feeling a difference in temperature. On a less permanent level, when your nose is blocked with a cold you may find that you can detect smells, although to a lesser extent, through your mouth.

Developing your senses will also help you with the skill of visualization, which is so important to successful spell casting.

During the course of this chapter we will look at each of the senses in turn, in terms of what the world is like without them and in terms of trying to use them to a greater extent. Then we will move on to some work on the sixth sense. Try to work through each of the exercises thoroughly; even though you may feel that you already know these things, you may be surprised at the extra skills you develop.

Visualization is one of the most essential skills to develop in order to work successful magic, but in order to do that we have to refine the use of our senses so that the images we visualize are as complete as possible.

SIGHT

As I have said, for humans, sight is the dominant sense. In many other mammals it is usually either hearing and/or smell which are dominant. It is surprising how many people will cross a road or walk out in front of a moving car which they can hear but not yet see. And a close friend of mine once stood with her back to a pet shop she was looking for yet couldn't find it, despite the chirrup of the caged birds and the combination smell of rodents and sawdust! This, of course, is in part because our heads are full of a great many things which are not directly related to our senses, like shopping lists, appointments, thoughts about friends and loved ones, etc.

PRACTICAL WORK 1

Whilst most of us may, thankfully, never have to discover what life is like without our sight, it is nevertheless interesting to experience this for a short period. Moreover, there are potential circumstances where it could be quite useful. I would recommend that everyone should be able to navigate their own home without the use of their eyes. You never know when there may be a power-cut, and should there be a fire it could save your life. If you can, arrange for a friend or family member to watch over you in this exercise to prevent you hurting yourself; if this is not possible then do not attempt to navigate your way down, or past the top of, any stairs.

First, without preparing yourself by checking out the route, close your eyes and move from wherever you normally sit to the doorway of your room. Go slowly with your hands in front of you, take small steps and try not to lift your feet high above the floor, to avoid treading on things. Notice how different this feels and your concerns about pieces of furniture, etc which may be in your path. Now, try the same exercise after you have thoroughly looked at the route you will be taking.

Once you have tried this then repeat the exercise with a longer trip, perhaps going from your bedroom to the bathroom or, if you are ambitious, from your bed to the front door. But this time, pause every few steps to use your other senses: listen carefully, what can you hear? Is there the ticking of a clock, the creaking of a floorboard, or door? Perhaps the low hum of a piece of electrical equipment? Can you feel a draught, or the flow of hot air from a heater? Also use your sense of

smell, as different rooms have different scents; the bathroom usually smells of soap, the kitchen of food, and so on. The room your pet sleeps in will often smell slightly of them. The average person's home contains a multitude of clues which do not require you to use your eyes to know where you are.

PRACTICAL WORK 2

To extend the information you obtain from your sight, try the following: find a location where you can sit undisturbed and, without drawing unwanted attention, watch people, preferably ones unknown to you. The window of a coffee bar looking out onto a busy street is good, or perhaps the window at your place of work in your lunch hour.

As you sit, observe those who pass by and see if you can work out what they are doing. Look at the way they walk; are they in a hurry, or at leisure? Do they swing their arms, keep their hands in their pockets, or clutch tightly to a purse, bag or case? Look at the expressions on their faces: do they look anxious, happy, frustrated, determined, etc? Do they look at those they pass, or avoid eye contact? Where you see two or more people walking together, see if you can work out their relationship: are they friends, a couple, a family, colleagues, etc. How do they relate to each other? Are they equal, or is one dominant over the other?

If you are able to make quick observations and deductions then you can also try this out in more social environments, which can allow you to compare what you see with what you hear, but do be careful you don't look as though you are actually watching people. If you can do this you will also become skilled at reading body language to the extent that you can tell when a person is not saying what they really mean or feel and, further, work out their true feelings.

developing the senses

PRACTICAL WORK 3

Of course the use of your eyes is not confined to observation of people. Make a point every day of looking out of your window at the world around you. Observe the sky, trees, plants and any wildlife you can see. Take a few moments to actually see what is happening, which direction the wind is blowing from, what kinds of clouds there are in the sky, whether any birds are flying or whether they are keeping close to the ground, and so on. From this, see if you can predict what sort of weather will be coming for your day.

the real witches' craft

PRACTICAL WORK 4

There is a very old party game which enhances observational skills. I was first introduced to it as Kim's game, but it has many other names. It is best played with at least two people. Take a tray, place on it ten to twelve unrelated objects, and cover them with a cloth. Remove the cloth for exactly one minute before covering them again, and get the other person to list the objects. It can be made simple for young players, with readily identifiable objects, like scissors, a spoon, etc. Or it can be made harder for older people by including more complex things like a strip of newspaper with a few random words, or an obscure piece of electrical equipment which they may have to describe. Or you can increase the interval between viewing the objects and recalling them. If the game is played frequently you will find that the mind's ability to take in, and then recall, a lot of visual information is greatly increased.

If you are working on your own you can do a similar exercise with a new magazine with a lot of pictures in it. Open it at random and give yourself a timed minute to examine a picture. Close the magazine and then write down as much as you can remember. It's best to do it in writing as just trying to remember can be very unreliable! Check your results against the picture. Of course, some illustrations will be better for this purpose than others; some may be too simple and others too well known. It can, however, be interesting to see how little of a familiar advert you can actually recall, even though you may have seen it hundreds of times before.

HEARING

Whilst you had a little experience of not having the use of your ears in the second exercise, a complete loss of hearing can be a quite different thing! Moreover, there is a considerable difference between being born deaf and going deaf at a later age. Both can be severe disabilities, but both can, and are, overcome by a great many people. For us hearing is important, but not as important as it is for many animals, like dogs. Our dog has extremely good hearing, which is not always an advantage as he starts to bark when he detects the postman's van, long before the postman pulls up outside the house! But hearing is not the only way we detect sound. Beethoven still composed music long after going deaf, because he could feel the vibrations that music made through the piano and the floor. Bats do not 'hear' as such but detect vibrations in the air, using a form of sonar. This is an important point which I will return to later; 'sound' is, like much of the essence of the world, a question of vibrations. Having said that, for our ancient ancestors, hearing was far more important, as not only would they use this sense to detect the presence of prey or the approach of predators, but it also played an important part in their magic. It is being discovered that a large number of sacred sites, especially those associated with caves, are linked to uncommon sound effects; places with special echoes and resonances. But to return to our sensory exercises in the here and now:

PRACTICAL WORK 5

It is relatively simple to experience the world without the benefit of good hearing, but much harder to achieve a complete absence of sound. However, purchase a set of earplugs from your local pharmacy. They will not block out all sound, so also place a set of headphones over them. This should reduce your hearing to the point where you can hear little, if anything. Spend an evening in your home doing all the things you would normally do, although if you use the radio or television, set the sound to a very low level before you plug your ears. If you do not live with sympathetic people, then try to do this on a night when you are likely to be alone. Make sure you do a series of normal activities, like having a bath (not a shower!), watching TV (especially your favourite programme), making dinner, and so on. If you can find a friend to help you, ask them to behave as normally as possible, and not to make allowances for your 'test'. Try to continue this for a couple of hours at least.

Once your test is completed, give some thought to and make notes on how you felt; in particular how you found yourself using your other senses. For example, if you felt the approach of someone else by the movement of air in the room, or how you found it more difficult to cook without using your hearing to tell you when the fat was spitting. Try to be aware of the ways in which your other four senses became more important to you; for example was your sense of smell more acute?

developing the senses

Today our ability to notice what we hear is compromised by the fact that we live in a very noisy world, and a lot of this noise is man-made. Even disregarding TV, radio and the like, there is the hum of the refrigerator, the cooling fan on the computer, the water heater, the clock, etc. Should you turn all equipment off there is still background noise: in a town or city there will be the almost constant sound of traffic, and even if you live in the country as I do then there is still the murmur of cars on a distant road and planes passing overhead. Of course, the world is never silent; there will always be the sounds of nature, but for most of us these sounds have just become background, and to make the most of our sense of hearing it is a good idea to learn how to tune back into these sounds.

PRACTICAL WORK 6

First, it is a good idea to learn to identify the background sounds in your daily life. Find a period of time when you can be alone in your room and turn off all sound-creating equipment, like TV, radio, CD player, etc. Lie down and close your eyes. Now listen carefully to the sounds around you. See if you can identify each, and work out which are from within the room, the home or from outside. If you can, repeat this in other rooms of the house, and take note of the difference from one room to another. On each listening occasion spend at least half an hour, as the longer you listen the more you will hear.

Now repeat the exercise outside, in your own garden or, if you can, in a place away from the sounds of modern life. While you are listening, try to visualize the scene around you. If you can hear the wind in the trees, where are they in relation to you? How far away? How tall? Are they in full leaf or partly leaved? Can you hear birds, or other animals? When you feel that you have as complete a picture in your mind as is possible, open your eyes and check to see how accurate you have been.

developing the senses

PRACTICAL WORK 7

Another way of extending the use of hearing is to watch a favourite TV programme with your eyes closed. TV is better than radio for this purpose as radio is designed to be a listening medium, whereas TV is designed to be visual so you will have to work that much harder to really use hearing in place of sight. As you listen to your programme, try to visualize the whole scene: location, props, characters speaking and perhaps any bystanders. You can open your eyes every once in a while to check your mental picture with the one on the screen, but try to limit this. If you do this regularly you should soon be able to visualize whole scenes quite accurately. When you feel that you have developed the skill with a programme you are familiar with, you might like to try it with another that you do not normally watch.

the real witches' craft

Remember that in all these exercises you are refining your skills with your senses, in order to become more aware of what is around you in daily life as well as to improve your ability to visualize. So in addition to writing down your thoughts and feelings after these exercises you might also try to be aware of any effects in your daily life. Many people find that they become more aware of what is going on around them, in particular they find after the hearing exercises that they become more aware of who is around them. This enhancement of the sense of hearing can be tested with a close friend: ask them to try to quietly walk up behind you, whilst you are otherwise occupied, and to see how close they can get before you notice their approach.

TASTE AND SMELL

The senses of taste and smell are closely linked; this is why food tastes different when you have a blocked-up nose. Those who live with cats may well have noticed that when a cat scents something really interesting it opens its mouth so as to appreciate the smell more. This is called flehming, and what they are doing is inhaling through nose and mouth at the same time, so that the scent particles can be tasted at the same time as smelt. Whilst a bit complicated for humans it is something that you can learn to do, although I'd advise not doing it in public until you have mastered it, as it can look quite odd! As an aside, this is a very good technique for detecting the quality of a wine, before you're committed to swallowing it!

Taste and smell are also very closely linked to memory. The scents of the seaside, freshly baked bread or new leather are just a few examples of smells which can transport us back to a specific moment in time. Similarly, the taste of certain foods can be equally evocative, perhaps reviving memories of childhood or a special occasion.

developing the senses

PRACTICAL WORK 8

It is easy to isolate your sense of taste from that of smell, simply by pinching your nose when eating something. Of course, if you have one of those nose clips worn by some swimmers, that's even better as it prevents you smelling things whilst you are preparing your tests and leaves both hands free.

Prepare a selection of foods including sweet, salty, bitter, sour flavours. By the way, if you are not sure about bitter and sour, then try separately the yellow peel and white rind of the lemon; this should remove all doubt! With your nose pinched or otherwise blocked, take tiny amounts of each substance and try it on varying parts of your tongue: the middle, the edges, the front and the back. Take a drink of water between each sampling to clear the palate. Note the differences not only in taste, but in strength of taste for each location. Also try substances with more subtle flavours, such as a couple of different types of bread or different types of olive oil – two or three types of freshly picked mint are another good challenge. Once you have tested two or three without your sense of smell, try them again, in the same sequence without impeding your nose, and again notice the differences.

If you can do so, try eating your favourite meal without the use of your sense of smell. You may be surprised at how bland it tastes, but persevere and don't submit to the temptation of adding any flavour enhancers to improve it.

the real witches' craft

It's a good idea to spread these experiments out over several days as your palate will become overwhelmed if you try to do this in one session.

Most people these days eat a lot of processed foods, and these contain high levels of salt, sugar, artificial sweeteners and other 'flavour enhancers' which not only interfere with our natural sense of taste, but can also contribute to all manner of bodily ills. Even if you shop carefully you may find that products labelled low in salt may have increased levels of potassium (which is but another salt) and those labelled low in fat or sugar may have increased levels of artificial sweeteners or salt added.

As with our other senses, today we are bombarded with so many artificial tastes and scents that our senses are dulled. The air we breathe may taste and smell of car exhaust, in our homes we have so many chemical cleaners that we may use other chemical 'air fresheners' to produce an agreeable smell. I certainly notice, when I visit a city, that the air is not the same, it smells and tastes of chemicals and it affects the way I perceive what I eat. Furthermore, in towns and cities people tend to wear more scented and perfumed products which also affect the way they are perceived. When I was younger it was a common tip for women going to job interviews to wear a male scent as this would subliminally incline interviewers to think of them as being 'stronger' and less feminine!

Probably one of the best ways of enhancing your sense of smell is to spend some time in a clean air environment. Instead of masking smells, try to eliminate them for a while. For a week, or two if you can, eschew as many scents around the home as you can: Hot soapy water removes most common household grime. Eco-friendly detergents are usually either unscented, or only lightly scented. A spoonful of washing soda added to your wash will enable you to use less laundry agent and less fabric conditioners. Put away all incenses, scented candles and the like. Change to unscented soaps, shampoos and other cosmetics, and reduce to an absolute minimum any personal fragrances you use. Avoid the use of artificial 'air fresheners' and products intended to make the home smell 'good'. Buy a couple of potted herbs instead; Rosemary, Thyme and Lavender are good examples of plants which will give a light fragrance without a sickening chemical undertone. If you have children or pets you may find it useful to lightly sprinkle some bicarbonate of soda onto carpets and furnishings before vacuuming as this removes smells from all kinds of fabrics. Open all the windows and let the air blow through your home for a few minutes every day; even if you live in the heart of a city there are times when there is less traffic passing, or a good cleansing wind blowing. Once you have eliminated the backlog of smells in the home you will be far better placed to exercise your sense of smell.

PRACTICAL WORK 9

Provide yourself with a selection of herbs, spices, and even flowers. If you can get a friend to do this for you so much the better, as you will not know what has been supplied in advance. Either with a blindfold, or with your eyes closed, smell these to see if you can tell which is which. Try this both inhaling through your nose only and then inhaling through both nose and mouth if you can. Notice the difference between both techniques for smelling.

- There are other places where you can exercise your sense of smell: In any supermarket which has separate counters for delicatessen, fish and meat, go and actually smell the air. You don't have to look like a dog on the trail, just inhale deeply and be aware of what you are smelling for a change. All the exercises related to the senses are not requiring us to perceive anything new as such, but are rather aimed at allowing us to be aware of exactly what it is we are sensing.
- Take a walk through your local park or woodland; notice the different scents around you. Try this at a dry time, after rainfall, when the grass has been cut.
- As you leave your house every day, take just a few moments to smell the air. Can you taste the onset of rain? Does the air taste sweeter than usual?

developing the senses

Remember to make notes on your thoughts and feelings and to practise, and soon you will find your awareness of the world increasing, along with your ability to link this to other events around you. You will also find that you are building a sort of storehouse of the senses which will become invaluable later on.

TOUCH

People are naturally very tactile; you only have to see how a new baby will grasp a finger to see how important contact is to people. This is the same with other animals; contact with other living beings is essential, even if they are not of the same species. This is one of the reasons why contact with a cat or dog is felt to enhance life and to speed recovery from illness or emotional distress. And if you live with animals, particularly mammals, you will notice that they too seek physical contact, between themselves and with us, especially when uncertain or stressed. This could be because there is a storm coming, or because there is upheaval in the home.

Of course, the sense of touch is not just perceived through our hands, we feel with the whole of our skin and this can actually influence our moods and emotions. We all know how uncomfortable it can be when we are too cold or too hot, or how miserable it can be to wear clothes which have got soaked through in a sudden downpour. But also clothes which are sensuous to the touch will make us feel sensual, those which are uncomfortable, restrictive or irritating can make us irritable and short tempered! The touch of the elements can also affect the way we feel; think of the pleasure of warm sun on the skin, especially when it is unexpected, or the feeling of wind or rain. If you are in the habit of walking barefoot, you will also be aware of how sensitive even the thick skin on the soles of your feet can be to just the tiniest piece of grit. One of the most pleasurable aspects of touch can be massage, if performed skilfully.

Loss of the sense of touch, which is thankfully rare, can be serious. Sufferers of some forms of leprosy have to be acutely aware of exactly what every part of their body is doing all of the time, and have to learn to visually check themselves to be sure that they have not injured themselves as even a small cut can become infected and result in the loss of, say, a finger or toe. Not only that, but without a sense of touch, even the simplest of tasks become extremely difficult.

PRACTICAL WORK 10

This is a quick exercise to give you some idea of just how important touch can be. Hold the fingers of both hands under a cold running tap for ten to fifteen minutes until you can barely feel them. Now try to do up the buttons on a garment or write your name. You will find that you have to really look carefully at what you are doing and concentrate hard to achieve your normal level of skill.

However, here we are more concerned with using each sense to the full, so the following are designed to help you become more attuned to your sense of touch.

PRACTICAL WORK 11

Walk barefoot around your home, first with your eyes open and then again with them closed. Use your sense of touch both through your hands and feet to detect the differences between one room and another. Feel for differences in the texture of the floor covering, for even the same carpet will wear differently in different areas. Feel for differences in wall coverings, and so on. Repeat this with bare arms and legs and see if you can detect the differences in air movement from one room to another, and even within the room itself.

If you can, try this also outdoors in your garden and in other natural locations. You don't need to walk about with your eyes shut, which would be risky, not to mention looking odd! Just try standing still in different locations to feel the movement of the air, and the touch of the elements on your skin.

Not only do we receive a lot of information about our environment through our sense of touch and our skin, but the skin itself reacts to seemingly unrelated factors in our lives. We not only get 'gooseflesh' when we are cold, but also when we are unnerved or feel that something is not 'quite right'. There is also that sensation of the sudden shiver, sometimes called the feeling that 'someone has walked over my grave', which alerts us to the possibility that something is amiss. We also refer to physical sensations to explain our intuitive feelings about others; from the phrase that someone 'makes the flesh crawl', to the instinctive revulsion we feel for a clammy handshake. These,

and other reactions related to the skin and the sense of touch, are the remnants of what used to be important survival traits, left over from the time when we were far more aware of and in tune with the world around us.

As we have seen in some of the earlier practical exercises, reducing the input to one or more of the senses frequently results in enhancing others. As I mentioned earlier in this chapter, it is said that some blind people can detect certain strong colours by touch; red being said to feel warmer, and so on.

PRACTICAL WORK 12

If you wish to test your sense of touch further, you could prepare a number of coloured cards and see if you can detect, by feel alone, which is which. Choose simple, bold colours such as red, yellow, green, blue, black and white, to start with. Although, if you feel really confident you could also include orange, purple, brown, gold and silver. Ensure all the cards are the same shape and size and that you cannot see the colour from the reverse. Shuffle the cards and with your eyes closed select one. Hold this in such a way that you can feel it with the whole of your hand, fingers, palm and all, and see if you can tell what colour it is. When you have made your decision, open your eyes and see if you are right.

From the perspective of the Witch, the sense of touch is used to help to detect illness as well as in some forms of healing.

The senses have long been thought to relate to the Elements in several different ways, probably the oldest of which is: Air – smell; Fire – sight; Water – taste; Earth – touch. In more recent times, this is sometimes changed to include the fifth sense as follows: Air – hearing; Fire – sight; Water – taste; Earth – touch, and Spirit – smell. However, I feel it can be a mistake to try to tie the senses and the Elements together too closely. The senses are what we perceive the Elements with, rather than extensions of them, and therefore it is more important to learn to utilize them fully.

FULL MOON RITUAL FOR OPENING THE SENSES

This Ritual has many similarities with the rite of Self-Blessing which you may have come across before. However its intent is somewhat different. As you move through the various steps it is important to bring to mind your experiences from the exercises earlier in this chapter.

In addition to whatever Altar equipment you normally use, have a separate small dish of water and some salt. As with all Rituals, ensure that you have prepared yourself and everything you will need, including some means of grounding yourself afterwards.

Create your Sacred Space in the usual way and then when you are ready to begin, add a small pinch of salt to the water in your dish, dip the forefinger of your strong hand into the water and say:

'I do bless and consecrate this water in the name of the Goddess and the God that it may open my senses to the wonders of their world. Blessed Be.'

Kneel before the Altar with the dish of salt and water within easy reach. Dip all the fingers of both hands into the water and say:

'Gracious Lady, Mighty Lord, bless my fingers and all my skin that I may fully understand the sense of touch.'

Touch the fingers of your left and right hands together and continue:

'May I learn to really feel your blessings and my contact with all that you provide. Blessed Be.'

Close your eyes, and say:

'Gracious Lady, Mighty Lord, open my eyes that I may truly see the wonders of your world.'

Dip your forefinger in the water and anoint each eyelid with the water, and say:

'May I see with truth and honesty. Blessed Be.'

Open your eyes again. Touch both your ears with your fingertips and say:

'Gracious Lady, Mighty Lord, open my ears that I may truly hear the sounds of nature and the world.'

Remove your hands and, using the forefinger of your strong hand, anoint each ear with a drop of the water, then say:

'Let me hear with clarity and understanding. Blessed Be.'

Place the forefinger of your strong hand over your lips briefly and then say:

'Gracious Lady, Mighty Lord, open my senses that I might taste the wonders of your creation.'

Dip your forefinger in the water and anoint the tip of your tongue, and then say:

'Let me taste truly and clearly. Blessed Be.'

Place the forefinger of your strong hand over your nose, and say:

'Gracious Lady, Mighty Lord, open my sense of smell that I might know the scents of your world.'

Dip your forefinger in the water and anoint your nose, and then say:

'May I learn to understand the true scents of life and the land. Blessed Be.'

Finally, dip your finger in the water and anoint your third eye. This is on the forehead just above and between your eyebrows. Say:

'All powerful Lady and Lord, bless my senses of touch, sight, hearing, taste and smell, that I might learn to use them fully to understand your ways.'

Anoint your third eye a second time and say:

'All knowing Lady and Lord, bless me, that I might learn day by day to walk your path.'

Anoint your third eye for the third time and say:

'All Mother and All Father, bless my sixth sense that, through use of the other five, I learn to develop and to trust it. Let me grow in your ways. Blessed Be.'

Remain on your knees for a few moments of contemplation before concluding your Ritual as usual, clearing away and writing up your notes.

the real witches' craft

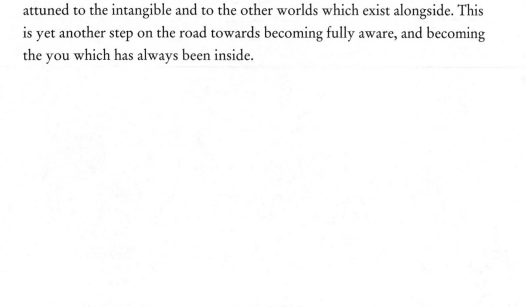

Learning to truly use, and then to expand the use of your senses will open your life in a great many ways. Not only will you become more aware of what is happening around you, but you will also find that you become more attuned to the intangible and to the other worlds which exist alongside. This is yet another step on the road towards becoming fully aware, and becoming the you which has always been inside.

Chapter Four

WAYS OF MEDITATION

Magic comes from within, not from the tools, equipment, candles, incense, and so on. In order to work magic, we need to be able to dismiss all external distractions and achieve mental stillness so that we are able to concentrate and focus properly. We also use meditation techniques to help in visualization, divination and pathworking techniques. These are all routes to access the Element of Spirit both within and without. Meditation is also helpful in our non-Craft lives as it enables us to clear the mind, is helpful in problem solving and helps us to relax. For some, the ability to meditate comes easily, but for most it is a skill which needs to be learnt and practised.

Before looking at developing this skill let's just clarify a few terms:

Relaxation – the ability to let the mind and/or body rest and to not allow worries and concerns intrude. For many people this tends to happen only during sleep, and even then our dreams are often indicators of what is on our minds, as we all find our thoughts returning to our current preoccupations. We even find it hard to physically relax, especially when there are chores or tasks we feel we 'ought' to be doing. It is worth noting that true relaxation is not the same as 'doing something relaxing'; really being able to relax means you can be comfortable doing nothing at all.

Meditation – the ability to focus on either nothing at all, or a single thing to the exclusion of all other thought. Most divination is done in a light meditative state, as this allows us to access our inner knowledge. Some people think that when meditating they will see, hear, or feel nothing of the outside world; this is not usually so, you will be aware of what is around you but it will not impinge on your mental state.

Guided meditation – the form of meditation when you listen to another who guides your thoughts in a particular way so as to facilitate meditation. This can take the form of a recording or it can be a narration, perhaps of a prepared 'story-line'.

Pathworking – this is a form of guided meditation where a 'story' is told which encourages the listener to consider themselves the central character. During the tale the listener is encouraged to take a journey where they will encounter certain signs, symbols, people or even God-forms. They will be encouraged to communicate with these, receive answers to questions or to interpret the symbols they see. Pathworkings may also be recorded, read aloud or, if you are on your own, then you need to recall the path and 'replay' it to yourself in your mind.

Daydreaming – this is when you relax and allow your mind to drift. Often you will find yourself in a scenario where you are interacting with others and the scene feels quite real to you. Daydreaming is quite similar to meditation, pathworking and indeed to visualization, the key difference being that it is uncontrolled and

unstructured. It can, however, be a good starting point to learning the other skills.

Visualization – this is the ability to create or to recreate a scene, set of circumstances, or even a function in such a way that it becomes 'real', and you can see, hear, taste, smell and feel it as though you were there. A key component of magic, visualization is dealt with more thoroughly in the next chapter, but is mentioned here because it follows on from the other meditation techniques.

As mentioned above, in the Craft we use meditation in a number of ways. It is a great way of clearing the mind of all the daily clutter. These days our lives are so busy that we rarely make the time to literally clear our heads. We all have worries and concerns which build up and which we should take the time to sort out, and as these accumulate it becomes harder to dismiss them and concentrate on the things which are really important to us. Having said that, it can be a mistake to try to go straight from a frantic day to a full meditative state, so it's a good idea to find a way of 'downloading' your concerns on a regular basis.

PRACTICAL WORK 1

Towards the end of the busy part of your day, perhaps after work or your evening meal, take a few moments to consider what has occurred. Make a list, either physical or mental, of the things you need to do to deal with any outstanding business. In the days when I commuted by train, I used to do this on the journey home. This is the time to consider any bills which need paying, birthday cards which need posting, etc. If you have had problems with your day-to-day relationships with others, this is also the time to consider whether or not you need to do anything to remedy these problems. Getting into the habit of this form of 'life-sorting' can be useful as it prevents things from building up. Once you have sorted your day, either deal with any outstanding business or firmly put these things to one side to be dealt with at the appropriate time.

If you can get into the habit of doing this daily, then you will find that it not only allows you to relax and to meditate, but also helps to make life in general a lot easier. Try it for a week and write up your general feelings about whether the exercise helps you to organize your life and clear your mind, rather than a day-to-day account.

One of the things often said about writers is that they can always think of a very good reason not to sit down and write! The same, however, can usually be said of anyone when it comes to finding time for yourself to relax in any way. There is always something more urgent, important, or which needs to be

completed before you can relax; be that the housework, tidying up, a call to a friend, or email to collect and answer! I imagine that many of you will have read the above exercise and thought 'I'll just finish this chapter and then give it a try.' One of the important disciplines of the Craft is to make yourself find the time, not just for reading but also for putting into practice that which you read about.

Having learnt to reduce the impact of daily life the next step is that of learning to relax fully. The next exercise is a technique developed from the practice of yoga. Because of its effectiveness it can be best to perform this last thing at night in bed, otherwise you could find yourself falling asleep at an inconvenient time or place. It has two parts, the first of which involves a breathing technique which is used to precede a lot of other exercises. Whilst you can practise this on its own, the second part of the exercise, that of muscle relaxation, will need the breathing exercise first.

PRACTICAL WORK 2

Part 1 - Breathing exercise

As a rule of thumb this usually takes about fifteen to twenty minutes to complete thoroughly, although with practice you will be able to achieve the same effect with only a few breaths.

Find a time and place when you will be completely undisturbed, make sure you are comfortably dressed, and not wearing any clothing which is in any way tight or restrictive. Lie down on your back in a warm and comfortable place, which is dimly lit, if at all. Cover yourself with a warm blanket and don't cross your legs or fold your arms. Close your eyes and breathe deeply, in through your nose and out through your mouth. Breathe deeply, evenly and slowly, filling your lungs fully. Breathe in to a mental count of three, hold the breath for three, breathe out to the count of three, and rest for the count of three.

As you breathe in, feel your lungs filling until your stomach rises – you may need to place one hand on your stomach temporarily to feel this, until you are used to the sensation. Continue breathing in this way until it feels natural and comfortable. Then think of the air you breathe in as being a pure golden light, and the air you breathe out as taking all your worries and cares away with it. Continue this slow breathing, filling your lungs with the golden light, then feel it moving down into your stomach. Then down each leg until it fills in each and every toe; take 4 or more breaths to fill each leg. Feel it driving out all aches and pains, and any illness. Feel the light moving down into each of your arms, right

down to the tips of your fingers, and driving out all distractions. Feel the light moving up through your neck and into your head, relaxing, calming and soothing you. Continue your breathing, focusing only on your breaths until you feel really relaxed and slightly 'floating'.

It may take more than one attempt to get the best out of this but it is well worth persevering. When you feel that you are successful you can either move on to part two of this section, or rub your arms and legs to bring you back to the here and now.

Part 2 - Physical exercise

On completing the breathing exercise you can move onto this physical relaxation which involves flexing various muscle groups throughout your body, and which you met in an earlier chapter. In some cases these may be muscles you are unaccustomed to moving on their own, and you may find it beneficial to practise these independently whilst in a position where you can actually see if they move or not.

Still lying warmly and comfortably on your back, wriggle the toes on one foot, then the other, then arch and flex each foot, rotate and flex each ankle. Now work your way up your body; tensing and relaxing each muscle group and moving each joint, one at a time, until you reach your head. Here you should move such of your features as you can; rolling your eyes and stretching your mouth. Finish by stretching and then screwing up your whole face. Finally, stretch your whole body slowly and gently, then relax again. As you go through these physical exercises, try to maintain the slow, steady breathing that you performed in part one.

At the end of this you may well find that you not only feel physically relaxed, but you may also feel far more aware of your body or feel a slightly 'floaty' sensation. If the latter is the case, don't immediately try to leap up and go about your day-to-day business without first grounding yourself. Make a point of noticing exactly how you feel at the end of the relaxation, and try to fix the sensation in your mind, so that you can recall it whenever you feel stressed or anxious. With a bit of practice you will find that you don't have to perform the full exercise to regain a sense of inner peace.

For many people it is far easier to learn meditation by focusing on one thing, rather than trying to focus on nothing, and over the years I have come across a number of recommended ways of practising meditation skills. Probably the most frequently mentioned is that using a candle flame.

ways of meditation

PRACTICAL WORK 3

Find a time when you can reasonably expect to be undisturbed for about twenty minutes to half an hour. Organize a space with as few distractions as possible. You will probably find it helpful if the room is dimly lit, and it may be useful to burn some relaxing incense. Take an ordinary white household candle in a secure holder, and light it. Place it in such a way that you can sit comfortably with the flame at eye level, about twelve to eighteen inches from your face. You may like to precede the candle-gazing with the above relaxation breathing (Practical work 2, part 1), or just take a few deep breaths to centre yourself. Rather than trying to drive out other thoughts, simply concentrate on the candle flame. Gaze into the flame, watch it carefully, focusing on its size, shape and movement. Observe also the halo of light around it. Let your mind remain only on the candle flame; if you find other thoughts intruding just bring your attention back to the flame. Try to attain this focus for just a few minutes at first, rather than for a longer time. If after about fifteen to twenty minutes you still feel you have not achieved anything, stop and return to the exercise another day.

Practise this two or three times a week until you find that you can lose all feeling of self whilst focusing on the flame. In other words, the candle flame is all that you are aware of, rather than being aware of yourself watching the flame. This is the first level of meditation, and must be fully mastered before you can move on to other levels. At this stage, you may also like to try visualizing a flame, rather than using the real thing. Some people actually find that it is easier to use a visualized candle.

Other techniques which you might like to try working with include:

- ❀ Hang a clear, faceted crystal in the window in such a way that the sunlight casts a rainbow onto the wall, and use this to focus on. Of course you can only do this during periods of reasonably continuous sunlight.
- ❀ Take a clear, faceted crystal and focus sunlight through it onto a large sheet of plain white paper. As above, you need sunlight for this.
- ❀ Fill a black bowl with water and look into its depths. You can also reflect a candle flame or the light of the Moon onto its surface. Many Witches use this as a method of divination, as well as meditation.
- ❀ Fill a wide, circular dish with sand and trace a spiral into the surface with your finger. Let your eyes and finger follow the spiral inwards and outwards, several times. Spirals have long been used in meditation and other-world experiences. You could also try creating more permanent ones by drawing, painting or other crafts.
- ❀ If you are lucky enough to have an open fire, then you can gaze into the flames.

As we are all different, it is worth trying out different methods to see which works best for you.

Once you can reliably enter this level of meditation, being successful say nine times out of ten, then you can extend the length of time. You will find that a deeper level or meditation comes with regular practice. Sometimes, this can feel like a sort of sideways 'slipping' feeling, rather like that which can happen on falling asleep and which wakes you up. If this is the case, don't worry, and

ways of meditation

don't try to force it, it's rather like approaching a nervous animal; the harder you chase, the more it runs away!

We also use a form of meditative state in the Craft when we practise divination. Whether we use tarot cards, runes, the crystal ball, dark mirror or whatever, it is the ability to detach our mind from the here and now and to dismiss conscious thought of the mundane world which enables us to do readings. It is a difficult state to describe, for on the one hand you are focused on the person, or problem, before you, whilst on the other you are able to screen out distractions from outside. This is akin to being able to take in information from both the inner and outer consciousness whilst tuning in and out between them at will. It sounds difficult but is in fact something we do all the time. We can drive a car and yet think of something else, or read a book whilst watching TV. It is simply a question of controlling the way we use these two parts of our mind.

PRACTICAL WORK 4

Choose a book which you find quite enthralling: it could be something you have read before or something new, fact or fiction; it doesn't matter so long as you find it really absorbing. Read until you get to a particularly fascinating part, and then save the book until you can find an equally interesting TV or radio programme to listen to. Combine the reading with listening, making yourself tune in to and out of first one then the other. With a bit of practice you should find that you are able to follow the thread of both, whilst not absorbing the background information, i.e. you grasp the plot but can ignore the descriptive aspects.

This ability to focus on more than one thing at a time is a very important life skill; at its simplest it means that we can talk to a friend whilst crossing the road safely. But in the Craft it enables us to focus on both the inner and outer planes at the same time, not only during divination but also when we are working magic, and during our rites and rituals. Equally important is developing the skill of being able to filter out distractions, otherwise your magic will be interrupted every time you have an incidental thought or hear a sound outside.

Moving on from meditation we come to guided meditation. There are many excellent recordings of specific meditations, but you can easily practise with any recorded story. You may feel that there is no need to practise listening to stories, after all, the majority of us first did this as very young children. But,

ways of meditation

as we grow older, we can easily lose the ability to completely immerse ourselves in a narrative. Also, being able to really enter a story is one of the ways of practising the ability to visualize. However, whilst stories or radio plays can be used to practise, they rarely result in a meditative state, so it is worth seeking out the opportunity to hear a proper guided meditation. Alternatively, use the following narrative. If you work with another person, then get them to read it to you, or you can record it onto a cassette yourself and then listen to it.

Guided Meditation - The Spring Path

Start by following the breathing relaxation earlier in this chapter, then, still lying down with your eyes closed, listen to the following and imagine yourself actually being the central character in the tale.

'It is a beautiful spring morning, the sky is blue and the sun is shining, it is warm but not yet hot, although the day promises much. There is a gentle spring breeze which you can feel on your face and in your hair. You are walking barefoot, slowly over fresh green fields. There are spring flowers all around and their scent rises as you step through them. The ground beneath your feet is cooling, soft and gentle. High above you a few birds fly, and you can hear them calling to one another. The land beneath your feet begins to rise in a gentle slope, and ahead of you is a small wood, a cluster of trees dense enough so that you cannot see to the other side, but not a forest.

It looks a magical place with shafts of sunlight dividing the cool shade into a magical and enticing place. You let your steps take you towards the trees: some are old but many seem quite young. There is Oak and Ash, Hazel and Rowan, Yew and Elm. There are also Holly and even a lone Willow. All are wearing the fresh green of new growth, making this

the real witches' craft

a truly magical place. As you approach you can see that the wood forms a crown on the top of the hill and in front of you, you see a pathway between the trees. You follow this path, noticing that, although the shade is cooler, it is still comfortably warm. The tops of the trees rustle in the light breeze, filling the air with whispers, and the song of the birds adds a music of its own. The scents are now those of woodland plants and warm moist soil. The path is clothed in a green moss, which feels soft and springy beneath your feet. There are ferns which brush against your legs, like the gentle caress of loving fingers. As your eyes become accustomed to the change in light you can see the flowers of the wood, small bright sparks of white, yellow and blue. These are the colours of the spring and the colours of the robes of the Goddess in her guise as Maiden. You pause for a moment to give thanks to Her for the wonders of the season.

As you start walking again you notice that the ground begins to slope downward a little and you follow it. Ahead of you the trees thin and there is a small clearing. Here, the sun shines through the break in the trees above, lighting a circular glade with a smooth grassy floor. Stepping into the glade you feel a deep sense of peace and contentment. All is quiet, even the sound of the wind in the trees seems to still. In the centre sits a grey boulder, about waist high. The rock is obviously very old, with moss and lichens growing on its surface. As you get closer, you can also hear the sound of running water.

Looking closely at the stone you see several markings etched into its surface and one of these is a spiral. You trace the spiral with your finger and as you do so you become aware of being watched from the edge of the trees. Looking up you see a young doe deer, only feet away from you. She stands still, quite unafraid, before turning and walking back between the trees.

Walking around the stone, you find a small spring bubbling from its base. The water from this forms a small pool, which is lined with small rounded stones of many colours. Kneeling, you dip your fingers into the water, and feel a tingling sensation as the icy water touches your skin. As you do this, a feeling comes to you that these waters are important, and you cup your hands and drink from the water. Although cold, it is the freshest, most wonderful thing you have ever tasted. As you swallow you feel it pass into your body, bringing a sense of being cleansed and restored. It washes away all doubt and anxiety, all care and worry, leaving you feeling completely at peace with yourself and with the world. Once again you give thanks.

Rising to your feet you notice that the Sun is now high in the sky. The morning has passed and it is now the middle of the day. You become aware that you can once again hear the sounds of birds in the trees, and the sounds of other creatures moving in the undergrowth. You also become aware that the scents of morning have now changed to those of a warm afternoon; they are richer and you can detect the warm, dark smell of the heated earth. Looking around the clearing, you fix its sights, sounds and smells in your mind, for this is a place you feel sure that you will wish to return to.

Now you retrace your steps, walking around the stone and once more you step onto the path between the trees. You walk back up the gentle slope, feeling more youthful and energetic than you did on your incoming journey. Stepping out from between the trees you look down over the fields, now in the heat of the Sun. There are bees and other insects taking nectar from the flowers as you make your way down the slope. When you reach the bottom of the hill, you close your eyes and take three deep breaths. As you release the third breath you return to the here and now. Open your eyes, sit up and rub your arms and legs to fully ground yourself.'

Sometimes on a guided meditation you may experience things which are not part of the narrative. These could be sights, sounds or scents, or you may even meet a person. Often you will be able to work out the meaning of these signs with just a little thought; they may relate to something in your daily life, or to something which has been on your mind recently. Sometimes, they may not be immediately clear. In either case, it is a good idea to record your experience in your journal as soon as you can, before you forget or subject them to interpretation. If you feel that you understand these insights, then note this as well. It is also a good idea to revisit these notes later to see if there are any alternative or deeper meanings. Many people find that the things they see and hear on a guided meditation can provide insights into personal problems or dilemmas in life.

Another way of using written meditations is to read them through several times, visualizing the narrative in as much detail as you can. When you have memorized the storyline, perform the breathing and physical relaxation and then visualize yourself actually taking the path from the meditation. Whichever method you use, it is important to read slowly and to allow the punctuation to guide the pace and to give emphasis to the reading.

The next form of meditation is Pathworking. Pathworking differs from guided meditations in two major respects. First the purpose: this is not simply to relax or regenerate personal energy, but to allow you to access the inner mind, to actively seek guidance from the divine or the subconscious, or to answer specific questions. The second is that there is a break or breaks in the narrative of a pathworking, where the subconscious mind takes over.

Because of these differences there are a couple of things you need to bear in mind when pathworking: where you have a particular question to ask it is important to form this carefully in your mind, so that it is unambiguous. For example, if you want to know whether to move home, then rather than asking, 'Should I move?', consider asking, 'How will it benefit me to move house at this time?' If you seek more general guidance, possibly from a God or Goddess form, then be prepared to receive information which may not be the answer you hope for. For example, the answer to the question, 'How can I have more money?' may come in the form of ways in which you could avoid spending! Quite often the answer may come in the form of a symbol, and its meaning may not be immediately clear. In these cases it is a good idea to make a note of the symbol and of anything around you in the narrative which seems significant, out of the ordinary or unexplained. Take some time to consider whether this symbol has any connection to your life and the things that are happening in your world. If this does not provide an explanation, then spend some time researching the meaning; quite often it is not the symbol itself which provides an answer, but rather it directs you onto a new path of exploration which has a deeper relevance. For example, a particular flower, say a yellow rose, may be relevant for its intrinsic meaning, that of friendship. In your personal life this could mean look to your friends for support. Alternatively, the yellow rose may be guiding you to look into the meanings of flowers and their healing properties as a new topic of study. Only you can determine the relevance to you of any particular symbol.

In the narrative for a pathworking you will find an instruction (or several) to wait, look around, or to pause. These are the times when you can expect to look for a symbol or to gain other understanding. In my texts this appears as '(Pause)' and you should give yourself at least thirty seconds of time before resuming the path. If you are reading a pathworking for a tape, or for someone else, then use a watch to actually time this, giving at least two minutes, as the break in the narrative often appears a lot longer to the reader than it does to the listener.

Should nothing seem to appear or to happen, do not try to force it, just relax and focus on your breathing. It can take more than one pathworking for many people to gain the full benefit of the experience. Sometimes this is because you are trying too hard to take everything in, or to derive meaning from everything around you; this is why it is important to relax into the

the real witches' craft

'story'. In other cases you may be looking so hard for something deeply significant that you overlook a more simple key.

To give you a feeling for the difference between guided meditation and pathworking I will repeat the spring path (above), this time in the form of a pathworking:

Pathworking - The Spring Path

Once again, start by following the breathing relaxation earlier in this chapter, then, still lying down with your eyes closed, listen to the following and imagine yourself actually being the central character in the tale.

'It is a beautiful spring morning, the sky is blue and the Sun is shining, it is warm but not yet hot, although the day promises much. There is a gentle spring breeze which you can feel on your face and in your hair. You are walking barefoot, slowly over fresh green fields. There are spring flowers all around and their scent rises as you step through them. The ground beneath your feet is cooling, soft and gentle. High above you a few birds fly, and you can hear them calling to one another. The land beneath your feet begins to rise in a gentle slope, and ahead of you is a small wood, a cluster of trees dense enough so that you cannot see to the other side, but not a forest.

It looks a magical place with shafts of sunlight dividing the cool shade into a magical and enticing place. You let your steps take you towards the trees, some are old but many seem quite young. There is Oak and Ash, Hazel and Rowan, Yew and Elm. There are also Holly and even a lone Willow. All are wearing the fresh green of new growth, making this a truly magical place. As you approach you can see that the wood forms

a crown on the top of the hill and in front of you, you see a pathway between the trees. You follow this path, noticing that, although the shade is cooler, it is still comfortably warm. The tops of the trees rustle in the light breeze filling the air with whispers, and the song of the birds adds a music of its own. The scents are now those of woodland plants and warm moist soil. The path is clothed in a green moss, which feels soft and springy beneath your feet. There are ferns which brush against your legs, like the gentle caress of loving fingers. As your eyes become accustomed to the change in light you can see the flowers of the wood, small bright sparks of white, yellow and blue. There are colours of the spring and the colours of the robes of the Goddess in her guise as Maiden. You pause for a moment to give thanks to Her for the wonders of the season.

As you start walking again you notice that the ground begins to slope downward a little and you follow it. Ahead of you the trees thin and there is a small clearing. Here, the sun shines through the break in the trees above, lighting a circular glade with a smooth grassy floor. Stepping into the glade you feel a deep sense of peace and contentment. All is quiet, even the sound of the wind in the trees seems to still. In the centre sits a grey boulder, about waist high. The rock is obviously very old, with moss and lichens growing on its surface. As you get closer, you can also hear the sound of running water.

Looking closely at the stone you see several markings etched into its surface. Study them closely, as one of these markings will have significance and meaning for you. Trace this marking with your finger and then watch and wait for a moment to see what may be shown to you.

(Pause)

the real witches' craft

Walking around the stone, you find a small spring bubbling from its base. The water from this forms a small pool, which is lined throughout with small rounded stones of many colours. Kneeling, you dip your fingers into the water, and feel a tingling sensation as the icy water touches your skin. As you do this, a feeling comes to you that these waters are important, and that they have the power to bring the answers to your questions or troubles. Immerse both hands into the water and ask for the guidance you seek, then reach down and take the first stone which catches your attention. Take it out of the water and examine it carefully, noting its size, shape and colour, for these will all have a meaning for you which will become clear with time.

(Pause)

Cup your hands and drink from the water. Although cold, it is the freshest, most wonderful thing you have ever tasted. As you swallow you feel it pass into your body, bringing a sense of being cleansed and restored. It washes away all doubt and anxiety, all care and worry, leaving you feeling completely at peace with yourself and with the world. Once again you give thanks.

Rising to your feet you notice that the Sun is now high in the sky. The morning has passed and it is now the middle of the day. You become aware that you can once again hear the sounds of birds in the trees, and the sounds of other creatures moving in the undergrowth. You also become aware that the scents of morning have now changed to those of a warm afternoon. They are richer and you can detect the warm dark smell of the heated earth. Looking around the clearing, you fix its sights, sounds and smells in your mind, for this is a place you feel sure that you will wish to return to.

ways of meditation

Now you retrace your steps, walking around the stone, and once more you step onto the path between the trees. You walk back up the gentle slope feeling more youthful and energetic than you did on your incoming journey. Stepping out from between the trees you look down over the fields, now in the heat of the Sun. There are bees and other insects taking nectar from the flowers as you make your way down the slope. When you reach the bottom of the hill, you close your eyes and take three deep breaths. As you release the third breath you return to the here and now. Open your eyes, then sit up and rubs your arms and legs to fully ground yourself.'

Once again, make notes on your experience as soon as you can, noting the things you saw, heard or felt as well as any interpretation you give them.

It is sometimes said that it is dangerous to stray from the path when pathworking. Certainly if you do so, you may well miss the intended object of your journey. Occasionally, you may even find yourself encountering things which you would prefer not to meet. This tends only to happen when there is something in your psyche which you are trying to avoid. If you feel able, it can be beneficial to confront such things, as otherwise they may well return on other occasions. However, if you feel really uncomfortable, then you have only to open your eyes, then sit up and rub your arms and legs in the same way as you would when finishing a pathworking.

If you are in the position of reading a pathworking for others, then it is a good idea to keep a look out for any signs of distress. Should you see anything which leads you to suspect that someone is perhaps experiencing difficulty, it is usually sufficient to insert the reminder that anyone experiencing any problem can simply open their eyes to return to the here and now. It is not generally necessary to bring the pathworking to a halt.

the real witches' craft

This once happened in a guided meditation group which I used to run, and I remember being a bit surprised that one individual did not choose to opt out even though she seemed to be quite uncomfortable. At the end of the meditation, which had been on swimming with dolphins, I asked her what, if any, problem had taken place. She told me that up until that point she had a fear of water and was therefore not comfortable being out of her depth, but that she had chosen to stay with the path in the hope that it would help her to overcome this fear. The last time I met her she was delighted to tell me that she had taken lessons and could now swim very well. This demonstrates another use for guided meditation and pathworking: that of using them to help to overcome fears and phobias. However, it is worth noting that the best way of doing this is to write your own narrative, so that you can control just how deeply you confront your fear before you enter a meditative state. If you are pathworking on your own, and feel at all nervous that you might find yourself in a difficult situation, then say the reminder out aloud to yourself three times before commencing your journey.

The Totem Animal Pathworking

Many Witches believe that we each have an animal form which is special to us. This is not a living animal in the way that a familiar is, but rather a spiritual animal form. It may be something which exists in the real world; a mammal, bird, fish, etc. Or it could be a mythical or fictitious creature. This is often referred to as a Totem animal. Seeing your Totem animal, whether in the world or in some other way, such as in a meditation, dream, picture or even on the television, is usually taken to be an indicator. What it indicates can be subject to the interpretation of the individual, much as the things seen, heard or felt in a pathworking are. Alternatively, if yours is an animal with its own folklore, such as the magpie, then you will also have this to draw upon.

If it is possible, perform this ritual whilst lying in the light of the full Moon. This need not be outdoors, as there is no sense in getting yourself chilled or soaked through! If it is not possible, go outside prior to the pathworking and spend a few moments gazing at the Moon and silently ask the Mother Goddess to guide you and give you her wisdom. Lie down on your back with your arms by your sides and your legs uncrossed. Make yourself comfortable, as any discomfort may well impinge on your thoughts. Ensure that you will be warm enough, perhaps by covering yourself with a blanket. Begin by performing the breathing and physical relaxation above (both parts of Practical Work 2 in this chapter).

'You are walking through the woods late at night, the air is warm and there is the gentlest of breezes moving the branches high above you. Whilst there are trees as far as you can see in any direction, they are well spaced and do not crowd around you. The light of the full Moon above you filters down through the trees, lighting your way. You are following a path which is soft and mossy beneath your bare feet. The path wanders gently to and fro in such a way that you cannot see where you are heading. As you walk you can smell the fragrance of the woodland and the deep musk scent of warm earth.

The path slopes downwards and here the woodland is obviously older, the trees are broader, their bark having moss growing upon it. Between them you glimpse the occasional fallen giant, some with fungus sprouting, providing shelter to many animals and insects. You look around as you walk, noticing the ancient trees of our land. Occasionally, you see signs of woodland creatures going about their nightly business.

As you follow the path downwards you can make out something ahead which glistens in the moonlight and you know that you are nearing your destination. But eager though you are, you still take the time to walk slowly and enjoy this time of peace and oneness with the land. You listen to the sound of the wind in the treetops and feel its gentle caress

the real witches' craft

on your skin. You feel the softness of the earth beneath your feet. Coming around a bend in the path you come to a break in the trees. Ahead of you there is a gentle grassy slope leading to a wide expanse of water. The smooth surface of the water has not a ripple on its surface and perfectly reflects the stars and moon in the clear night sky.

You walk to the very edge of the water and gaze at the reflected Moon, taking deep breaths of the warm night air. A movement on the far bank attracts your sight and, looking up, you see a figure on the other side. As soon as you see her you realize that this is the Mother Goddess. She shines, as with an inner light, and her robes of deepest blue seem to also reflect the stars above. Her face is full of the wisdom of the ages as she smiles encouragingly at you. Around her feet there is a light mist which swirls and eddies. In the mist you can see shapes almost form before fading away. You watch as the Goddess raises her arms towards you in a blessing. When she lowers them you notice the mist at her feet thicken, and then part, revealing a creature standing at her feet. At a movement from the Goddess, the animal moves forward until it stands at the very edge of the water opposite you. Take time to look carefully, and to observe everything about this creature; its size, colouring, eyes and the expression on its face.

(Pause)

When you are sure you have committed every detail to memory, give thanks to the Goddess for revealing your Totem animal to you. Once again she raises her arms in blessing and whilst she does so the mist thickens around her and the animal, until both are hidden from view.

Now is the time to retrace your steps through the forest. Return the way you came, walking slowly and holding the image of your Totem animal in your heart. When you are ready, open your eyes and rub your arms and legs to bring you back to the here and now.'

Write up your experience as soon as you can, noting all the details of your Totem Animal. If you can, it is a good idea to draw a sketch, even if your artwork is more diagrammatic than literal, as this can often help to fill in details which might otherwise have been lost. Try not to impose any prior knowledge of the creature on your recollection; it can be easy to allow your conscious mind to override your actual experience. If, for example you saw a large black bird which looked like a raven, but which had a white mark on its wing, you could be tempted to assume it was a magpie. But this may not necessarily be the case, it could be a raven with a white marking, and that marking may have its own significance.

If your creature is something with which you are not familiar, then the next step will be to see if you can identify it. Public libraries are excellent for this, as you can browse books on the natural world or books of mythical creatures without the need to spend a fortune on books. The internet, despite its usefulness in other respects, is not the best place to locate a match for an image you have in your mind unless you already have a shrewd idea what you are looking for. If you find a picture of your Totem animal, it is a good idea to get a copy to keep in your journal, or even to hang on your wall.

One thing to be a bit cautious of is if you see a present or past pet as your Totem animal. Whilst this could be the case, you may wish to repeat the pathworking at the next full Moon just to check whether it is not your subconscious trying to alert you to something connected to a current companion animal, or simply wishful thinking on your part.

Once you have identified your Totem animal, keep a watch for its appearance in your life. Often the appearance of your Totem animal, in any form, indicates that something special is about to occur, or alternatively that there is something you should be aware of. Note these appearances in your journal, as sometimes it can take a while before you fully understand the meaning of different kinds of sightings. There may be significance in the direction it faces or appears from, or it may be that the number or expression of the animal indicates something particular. Many Witches will call upon their Totem animal to accompany them, in spirit form, on their other-world journeys.

Just occasionally, a Totem animal is not one which occurs either in nature or in mythology. Should this happen to you, then you may wish to perform some meditations on your creature. Perhaps you could even write a pathworking of your own, where you can meet with it and ask it questions about its nature and meaning. In such cases you will be unlikely to see it in daily life, but you may find that, as you come to learn more about it, you become aware of its presence close by from time to time.

Just about any spell can be performed using meditation techniques, so long as you are sure that you can maintain your focus. In fact, this is probably one of the most common methods of solitary workers. Some Covens also use guided meditation and pathworking as a way of spell craft, although it can take some practice before everyone can contribute fully and in concert. Later in this book, I will discuss the creation and use of an Astral Temple, which is a permanent working place on the psychic plane, for acts of magic which are performed in a meditative state.

But in order to develop meditation and pathworking into truly useful tools for magical working, we need to take them to the next stage; that of visualization.

ways of meditation

Chapter Five

VISUALIZATION

In the last chapter I defined visualization as the ability to create or to recreate a scene, set of circumstances, or even a function, in such a way that it becomes 'real', and you can see, hear, taste, smell and feel it as though you were there. But that really only scratches the surface. Visualization can take you to other worlds: It can take you back in time to revisit events in your own past, or forward to see what might happen. It can take you to times and places which you have never experienced. It can even take you inside physical processes, such as healing.

When you visualize fully you actually move your mind from the 'you' of the here and now to another plane of existence. In the beginning you may have to think hard to really be in your visualized surroundings, to imagine the feel, scent and taste of the air. You may have to use a combination of imagination and memory to feel the ground beneath your feet, and so on. But as you practise, you will find that you really feel these things, to the extent that you actually become a part of the other environment. When this happens it is true visualization. It is like the difference between an ordinary dream and a really powerful one which leaves you so disorientated upon waking that you are not sure where you are.

The ability to visualize really is one of the keystones of magical practice. As Witches we can use visualization to determine the potential outcomes of a spell or magic, not just whether it will work but what ramifications or side effects it may generate. This helps to avoid doing spells which bring about unintended or wrong results. Remember that much mentioned phrase, 'be careful what you wish for, for you just might get it!' Witches also use visualization in the actual working of our magic. Probably the most quoted definition of magic is 'the ability to create change through use of will power', but in actual fact it could better be termed 'the ability to influence reality in accordance with the laws of nature'. This is why magic works best when applied to things which are based in nature, for instance, why you can work a spell to find work but not to make money. Work, or the exchange of energy to bring about benefit, is a natural concept; the tiger chases its prey to gain its dinner. Money, however, is a man-made intermediary in the exchange of energy, and not something which exists in the natural world. In addition to this, when working a spell which is directly intended to work on a natural process, it is more than a little helpful to understand that process. For example, healing spells are far more effective if you have a basic understanding of the actual healing process you are seeking to kick-start or accelerate. Being able to visualize those processes will make your magic work that much more easily and effectively. This works with any form of spell; the more clearly you can visualize the desired changes taking place, the better and more accurately the spell will work.

PRACTICAL WORK 1

Sit somewhere warm and comfortable and allow yourself to relax, perhaps performing the breathing exercise from the previous chapter. Think back to a really strong and happy memory. This could be a day in your childhood, when you were carefree and happy, or a more recent event. Whichever you choose, immerse yourself in this memory. Think about it in detail, and ask yourself the following questions: What was the weather like? What were you wearing? Who was there? Can you remember any scents, tastes? Explore the memory as fully as you can without forcing it.

When you feel that you have remembered it as completely as you can, open your eyes and make your journal notes. Consider whether you have remembered more than you expected to, or less. Record how you feel in the aftermath of the memory, as this can also be important. Sometimes vivid memories, even though of happy times, can bring about quite unexpected emotional responses, such as sadness or regret.

Using the same technique, perform a comparative exercise, selecting a memory from the past few days.

the real witches' craft

PRACTICAL WORK 2

Is your recent memory as complete as the one which you selected deliberately? Most people find that it is not. This is partly because your chosen memory from the past was a significant one. But it is also a direct result of the fact that as we get older our lives, generally speaking, become more cluttered and, unless we actually make a point of preserving our observation skills, we naturally become less observant. As we saw earlier in this book, there is much about our surroundings which we do not notice properly and recall unless we practise. Likewise, most of us were better at visualization when we were younger. This is partly because of the state of receptiveness of our minds and, for those of us who are older, partly because there used to be a greater emphasis on spoken and written narratives, i.e. radio and books, rather than TV and film. Therefore, one of the easiest ways of encouraging your ability to visualize is to listen to radio plays and recorded books, and to read. This may sound simple, but it can be surprisingly helpful in retraining your mind to visualize the scenes you read or hear in any detail.

PRACTICAL WORK 3

Find a work of fiction which contains a fairly substantial amount of description – in the words of Alice (in Wonderland) 'one with no pictures and few speech marks'! It's best if this is not a story which you are familiar with, as it can be all too easy to skip parts of a story you know. It's also best if this is something which has been written in the third person, so that you are not encouraged to consider yourself as a part of the story. You may also find it helpful if it is set in a time and place where you feel comfortable, rather than a totally alien environment, although if you enjoy science fiction, there's no reason why it shouldn't work for you.

Set aside a portion of time every day, where you can read a chapter at a time. In the case of a radio serial or audio-story this will be one episode at a time. In either case also set aside fifteen or so minutes afterwards to consider it. It's important to break the story up in this way to give you the chance to deal with it in manageable segments.

Try to visualize the characters and their setting as though you were there as an interested bystander. After each chapter spend a few moments in meditation on the story. Consider what else might have been happening outside of the main story-line; for example, if a scene is set at a market place, what kinds of stalls were there, who was running them, what were they wearing, and so on? Try, in your mind's eye, to expand the scene as much as you can. During your meditation you may find that the story progresses further than the point at which you left it in reality. Should this occur then relax into it and allow it to flow. Later you can compare your 'story-line' with that of the author.

When making notes in your journal, remember to focus on how your ability to visualize increases, rather than the actual content of the story you are following. During the same period as working on developing your ability to visualize fictitious scenes, although obviously not at the same time, you can also expand upon your ability to use recall to visualize things from the real world.

In our daily lives we spend much of our time going to places with which we are quite, or very, familiar, but which are not under our personal control, like shops, school, work, or the homes of friends or family. However often we may visit such places we have no idea whether changes may have been made in the way things are placed, the furniture or even the décor. Many of you will be familiar with the slight irritation caused when your favourite convenience store inconveniently alters the arrangement of goods on the shelves! Or the disconcerting feeling you get when visiting someone you know well who has, without warning, moved all their furniture around. This is because, consciously or subconsciously, you have already visualized how things will be when you get there. In the case of the convenience store you may even have planned your shopping list with the store's layout in mind.

visualization

PRACTICAL WORK 4

This exercise is one you can try perhaps once or twice a week, but don't try to do it for everywhere you visit, or you will soon drive yourself, not to mention most of your friends and acquaintances, to distraction!

Before setting off to visit somewhere you go reasonably often, take a few moments to close your eyes and picture it. As before, try to recall as much as you can: the physical layout, the sights, sounds, scents, and so forth. If you can, include in your mental image the people who will be there, what they will be wearing and doing.

When you arrive at the location, bear your visualized image in mind and make mental notes of any differences. Try to work out whether it is your memory which was adrift or whether any changes have actually taken place.

It's worth mentioning that this exercise is also used when learning to practise astral travel.

Like many of the other skills covered in this book, visualization comes easily to some people, but most need to work at it, although with practice, it does become easier. However, there are some interesting indicators as to whether an individual may find it easy or not. Those who spent a lot of their childhood reading or having to amuse themselves without technological amusements often find it easier. Now you may feel, especially if you've heard me speak on the subject, that this comment comes from a somewhat 'luddite' approach to technology! But it is true that one of the side effects of living in a world where we have access to constant stimulation in the form of umpteen television channels, computerized games and so on, means that we rarely have to fall back on our own thoughts in order to exercise our minds. It is the absence rather than the presence of external stimulation, which enables the mind to develop, or to put it another way; boredom can be good for the mind!

Whilst on the subject of the workings of the mind, it is worth mentioning that there are large areas of the brain whose functions are not really known and some well-respected scientists feel that these areas may have unrecognized talents and abilities. From this we can ponder on the possibility that there may yet, one day, be a scientific explanation for some of the occurrences we call magic. Of course, from our perspective it is sufficient for us to know that our magic works; we are somewhat less concerned as to whether or not it can be explained or proven. But who knows what the position could be in, say, twenty years time?

visualization

PRACTICAL WORK 5

As mentioned before, visualization is in many ways a form of controlled day dreaming. So in this exercise you are going to design your own daydream and then visualize it.

Imagine a 'perfect' day: Start by deciding on the location; perhaps a beach, or the countryside. What is the land like under your feet? What sort of views are there? Are they flat or hilly? What can you see in the distance, and so on? Consider the weather or climate. Is the sky clear and blue, or are there clouds? Is it warm or hot, is there any breeze? What time of day is it, and what is the position of the Sun and/or Moon? Are there other people around? Will there be sounds around? And what about scents and smells? Try to incorporate factors which relate to each of the five senses. And yourself, what are you wearing? Are your feet covered or bare? And, most importantly, why have you come here? Is this a favoured memory? Have you come to achieve something particular, or just to relax? Give some thought as to whether you want to start your daydream by your arrival at the location, or whether you will just be there. Fill in as much detail as you can, changing things to suit your idea. Take your time over this, possibly making rough notes as you go.

Once you have designed your daydream, consider whether there are any practical steps you can take to aid your visualization. For example, if your setting is a warm day, but the actual weather is cold, then turn the heating up a bit. Likewise, if it should be sunny, then turn the lights on. If there are particular scents which you can include then do so, for example a few warmed pine needles can be evocative of a forest, or some dampened seaweed or shells will help to recall the beach. If you have any CDs or cassettes of natural sounds without words, such as are often sold for relaxation, these can also be played very quietly in the background.

Set aside a reasonable period of time when you know you will be undisturbed. Don't attempt to cram this into a short fixed time, as you will feel pressured. Once all is ready, and assuming you feel in the right frame of mind, then settle yourself comfortably, perform the breathing exercise and start by imagining the scene you have created for yourself. Allow the scene to develop, don't worry if it departs from the one you planned, but just enjoy the experience.

One of the things which concern many people is how to tell the difference between imagination and the point where 'true' visualization takes over. Or the point at which you are consciously controlling the images in your mind and the point at which the subconscious, or psychic ability, takes over. There are no hard and fast ways of telling the difference as the whole is more like a scale of grey shades than a black and white boundary. Some people describe the difference as a sort of side-slip which moves them from one level to another. Others say that there is no perceptible change-over point, but that you know afterwards how deep your meditation or visualization has been. Personally, I have found that either description can apply at different times. However, wondering about the level of your meditation or visualization whilst it is in progress will almost certainly prevent it from working, so it is better to focus on your intent rather than anything else. After all, most of us do not fully understand how the television works, but that does not prevent us from using it. In the same way as working spells and magic, the best way of

visualization

knowing when your visualizations work, will almost certainly be by looking at the results.

As I mentioned earlier, Witches often use visualization prior to working magic, to determine whether there may be any unintentional or unwanted results, or side effects, of the spell. For example, if you work magic to protect your car from burglary, you could do so by making it not seen by those with bad intentions, or who are not honest. However, it doesn't take a great deal of imagination to work out that many people have times when their intentions are not all that they should be, and that this probably includes drivers. The result? You may well have made your car not obvious to a large number of other road users, which is obviously not a safe way to be driving around! Visualization may well throw up this unwanted side effect of your spell and allow you to reword it to make your car, and its contents, undesirable to thieves and vandals. Alternatively, consider the ubiquitous love spell: if you work magic to make someone love you, it may satisfy your desire in the short term, but as sure as the Goddess made little green apples, the day will come when you are asking yourself whether their love for you is real, or just the result of magic, complete with the resultant loss of self-esteem. Yet another example lies in healing: if a person has a broken leg then removing their pain will enable them to use that leg and they will probably do themselves more harm without feeling it.

So you can see that, whenever you are thinking about working any spell, however seemingly innocuous, it is as well to consider what the results may be. If you put as much care and preparation as possible into this, then you will be able to meditate on the spell and visualize the results, which will bring about a much greater and more thorough understanding of its potential.

the real witches' craft

PRACTICAL WORK 6

Think back over some spells you have already performed, although not too recently, say within the last couple of months but not within the last few days. Find yourself some personal space and visualize yourself doing one of these, in as much detail as you can. If you have kept a journal of your workings you should be able to look it up prior to the visualization to jog your memory. Try also to recall your state of mind, what were your thoughts about the spell and what did you truly hope for at the time, which is not always the same as your stated intent.

Next, using your knowledge of the actual results of this spell, set yourself to visualizing all the possible results, even those which may yet come to pass. Compare your visualization of the outcome(s) with your hopes for the spell. If at this point you have concerns about the spell you might want to rework it (if necessary take a look in the final chapter which includes information on cancelling spells).

Don't forget to make notes in your journal, for this and all the practical work you do, as there may yet be effects of that magic which you have not discovered.

Of course, a lot of the potential outcomes of any spell can be deduced by a little careful thought and some knowledge of human nature. Whether the process of visualization actually gives the answers in and of itself, or whether

it simply allows us to unlock our inner knowledge of the way the world works, is a debatable point. But like many other things in the magical realm, we can still use the process, whether we understand precisely how it works or not.

Visualization for Spell-working

Moving on from visualization before working magic, we come to the use of visualization as the spell-working itself. A good while ago, in a 'previous' (i.e. non-writing) life, I used to train salespeople to sell. The company I worked for at the time had very formal methods for such training and one of the techniques they told us to teach was to 'visualize the sale'. This involved the salesperson thinking through all the steps of selling, from arriving at the company's car park through to shaking hands on the deal. Each step was to be imagined in as much detail as possible, complete with details of the office they would meet the client in, polite conversation, and so on. Now for you and me, this is obviously no less than a form of spell-working, something I have no doubt they would have been horrified to learn!

When using visualization to perform a spell we are simply thinking through all the steps in the change which we wish to manifest, but we are doing so within the Circle, whether it be formally cast or created on the psychic plane. We are also utilizing the energies and the balance of the Elements to make the change happen. For this reason it can be helpful to think through the steps necessary between 'things as they are' and 'things as you will them to be'. For example, if your spell is to heal an infection you could think through the actual healing process, of white blood cells gathering to fight the infection and removing the cause of it. In a spell to meet a soul mate, you might start with getting ready to go out, followed by visualizing meeting someone and getting on really well. The key lies in the detail, the more you can 'see' happening the more easily the spell will work. In the oft cited example of finding a car parking space; the more clearly you can visualize where the space will be found, and possibly even the previous occupant driving away as you arrive, the better the magic will work. This doesn't mean you have to have a complete knowledge of every process for which you craft a spell, but rather it means that the more information you have, and use, the easier it is to produce a spell which will have the desired effect.

Many Witches find that the process of designing a spell actually starts the magic even though they may have intended to perform the magic at a later point. Certainly, I find this when preparing spells and rituals for Coven use, as the focus required to set them into writing, so that the whole group knows exactly what they are doing, is quite often enough to set the magic into motion. Having said that, I would always still go through with the act of magic, to give maximum impetus to the spell.

The way in which the preparation of the spell actually starts it working is another reason why it is essential to think through your magic very carefully before you start. Otherwise, you could set things in motion which you subsequently want to change. I am sometimes asked if it is possible to work spells without meaning to, particularly when you feel very strongly about something, or if it is possible to 'hex' someone by 'accident'. The short answer is, technically speaking yes, but it does not happen very often. This is because in order to work magic you need to be in balance, which you are unlikely to be if you are in the grip of say anger or outrage. Having said that, you should always try to keep your magic separate from uncontrolled emotions, and to be aware of the times when you might be tempted to let rip with something you may later regret. It is sometimes said that no-one ever prospers who crosses a Witch; perhaps this is at least partially explained by acts of inadvertent magic, or perhaps it is simply the way that the Craft looks after those who follow it.

When you first begin visualization exercises you will almost certainly find it easier to work with your eyes closed, but as you practise you will find that you are able to visualize with them open. Whilst this is not essential in every

visualization

case there are times when this ability is more than a little useful; remember that car parking spell? When you visualize with your eyes open, most people find that what they see can be compared to seeing a film projected onto a clear screen. The image is there, but faint and superimposed over reality. It needn't prevent you from being completely aware of the real world in any way, even though you are actually present in two different realities. This is sometimes referred to as walking in both worlds. However, if you find that your visualizations are in any way distracting, then please make sure that you don't try them when driving or in other risky circumstances.

Those of you who have done some group working may in fact be used to certain forms of this, such as visualizing the pentagrams you draw when invoking the Elements. These visualizations become, with practice, more than just images in your own mind, they become visible to others. One of the exercises I often practise with my Covenors is that of learning to create pentagrams in such a way that others can see them. If you have a fellow Witch to work with, you may like to try the following:

PRACTICAL WORK 7

One person leaves the room. The other then invokes one of the Elements of Air, Fire, Water or Earth, describing its pentagram in the air. They must do this silently, as even the quietest whisper can often be picked up by the subconscious. The person returns to the room and has to detect, or see, which element has been invoked. The 'test' can be made easier by placing the pentagram in the correct quarter, and/or in the right colour, or it can be made harder by leaving out these correspondences. Don't forget to banish each Element after each part of the exercise!

Of course, you can try this exercise with other visualizations if you wish, but the four Elements make a good starting point.

One of the great advantages of using visualization as a magical technique is that you can do it anywhere, regardless of who may be about. This means that your magic can be done as soon as you become aware of the need. You can also use it for spells which would otherwise be very difficult to carry out, e.g. a spell protecting the boundaries of your home can be very complicated if your house adjoins other properties. But if you are visualizing you can 'walk through walls' and traverse other people's land with no risk of being seen.

For many Witches visualization spells make up more than half of their magical workings, whether they're at home or not. Of course, for any act of magic you need to bring the Elements into balance, but this can also be done using visualization alone. In the early days of developing this technique you may have to visualize yourself performing the same actions and saying the same words as you would normally do, but, as outlined in chapter 1, with practice you will find that you simply have to briefly focus your thoughts on the Element for it to be invoked. If you are not yet confident that you can do this reliably then have some more practice before trying your next Ritual.

Defensive Visualization

Most Witches protect their homes against physical and psychic troubles, by creating a magical boundary around the edge of the property. It is intended to deflect the attentions of burglars, those who might deliberately ill-wish any of the family and more generalized negative feelings and energies. There are many ways of doing this; perhaps using salt and water or even iron filings to mark the boundary. This magical boundary should be reinforced regularly to keep it strong. The focus of the following Ritual is the creation of such a defensive boundary, but you could easily substitute any magical working which you need to do at this time, so long as you work it through visualization.

Settle yourself comfortably in a place you would normally use for your spells; I usually prefer to sit cross legged on the floor. Visualize your altar and any tools you would usually place on it, including salt, water and an Asperger. Use visualization to invoke the Elements, to invite the Goddess and the God, and to cast the Circle.

Now in your mind, add some salt to the water and consecrate it. Offer it up to the Goddess and the God for their blessing. Now, still visualizing, walk the bounds of your property, going deosil, and sprinkling a little of the salt water as you go. As you sprinkle the water, it becomes an electric-blue light forming a barrier which completely encloses your home, allowing nothing negative to affect anyone who lives there. When you have completed your circuit, watch as the boundary rises up to complete a sphere of protection.

As you are using visualization you can travel within any walls between your home and your neighbours', and you can walk over any hedges or walls outside, ensuring that you cover the entire external boundary.

When you have completed your protection, remove the Circle, banish the Elements, and thank the Goddess and the God, all through visualization.

Visualization makes magic actually happen, and it is one of the most important steps in advancing your magical practice. Together with the other skills it allows us to start using and hence developing the sixth, or psychic, sense.

visualization

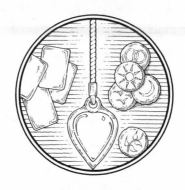

Chapter Six

DEVELOPING THE SIXTH SENSE

In chapter three we looked at the five 'normal' senses of sight, hearing, taste, touch and smell, with a view to preparing ourselves to develop the sixth sense. But what is the sixth sense? Well, it's defined as 'the ability to perceive that which lies beyond the powers of the five senses' (Chambers Dictionary). In other words, the sixth sense covers those things which we know but did not detect through our five senses.

Of course, there are some people who would deny that there is any such thing as a sixth sense, that it's just coincidence or even, in some cases, trickery. Others feel that it is more likely that it is our subconscious which provides us with such information; that we actually see and hear a lot more than we are actually aware of. Indeed, this is one of the more common explanations for some of our dreams; that our minds are actually sorting and collating the information they received both consciously and subconsciously during our waking hours.

Personally, I feel that whilst we do learn a lot from the information gathered by our subconscious, there is still definitely a part of our mind which gathers information which cannot be explained away. And experience leads me to believe that this part of the mind is available to everyone, although for many it lies dormant most of the time. Part of the reason for this dormancy stems from in our early years; certainly when I was younger I was actively discouraged from any display of 'intuition'. If I 'guessed' who was about to phone, or who we would meet on a shopping trip, my mother would shush me firmly, although it was she who taught me to read the tea-leaves as a child. Whilst many parents these days don't have quite the same attitude, there is still a definite underlying attitude that such things are not to be encouraged. You only have to watch any TV programme to become aware that displays of your sixth sense may well result in you being investigated, or treated as a laboratory guinea pig! These attitudes are also reinforced by the fictions which almost always put the owner of such 'powers' in jeopardy from dark forces! In addition to this, education systems around the world give a definite emphasis to those things which have been already proved scientifically. Whilst I have no problem with that as a concept, it can be somewhat disconcerting to realize that many things are not accepted as scientific fact until years, and in some cases decades, after they have been thoroughly investigated, and even then it can take a goodly time before they are taught in schools. Even then, some authorities can choose to ban the information like, for example, those schools who still refuse to teach theories of evolution.

So perhaps it is as well to start this chapter with the suggestion that possession of a sixth sense is more than likely the rule, not the exception. Should you be aware of things which come under the heading of the sixth sense, this is more likely to be normal than in any way unusual. To put it flippantly: the good news is that your sixth sense is alive and working just fine. The bad news is that you may well have forgotten, or not learned, how to use it!

Divination and the Sixth Sense

Now, divination is one of the more obvious examples of the sixth sense. Learning to read the Tarot, runes, dark mirror or crystal ball is recommended to those who are starting out on many of the Pagan paths. And many 'new Witches' will acquire one, or more, of the tools of divination quite early on in their exploration of the path. However, there is a huge fall-off rate in these, and probably nine out of ten Witches will have a pack of something or other tucked away unused in a drawer somewhere! But why unused? Well, there are a number of basic obstacles in the way of learning divination, whatever the technique.

First, many divination tools, such as Tarot and runes, come with a little booklet. At first sight this would seem to make interpretation easier, after all each card, rune or whatever is given its own meaning. However, the task of learning, say, the meanings of all 22 runes, in both upright and reversed configurations, is quite daunting enough, let alone those for all 78 tarot cards! If the included little booklets are not enough, there is also a wealth of books written on the subject of divination in general as well as for specific divinatory techniques. A good many of these will contradict each other, and some are very definitely written from somewhat unusual perspectives. I recall a decidedly Christian interpretation of the Norse runes as being quite off-putting when I first looked at it. But even if you overcome these obstacles, then you will almost certainly discover that the meanings are at best obscure and at worst irrelevant to the subject you are seeking to divine. In other words, the interpretations themselves need interpreting, and to make matters worse, you still have to interpret each card, rune or whatever in combination with the others that turn up in your reading. Then, of course, there are some divinatory tools which come with little or no 'helpful' advice; the dark mirror and crystal ball are examples of these. I remember once being approached by someone interested in buying a crystal ball who asked, 'Where's the switch to turn it on?' It's no wonder that some tools end up being consigned to the back of a drawer.

Secondly, as mentioned above, our minds these days tend not to be open to the whole concept of divination, as the denial or rejection of any form of psychic phenomena is very deeply ingrained in our upbringing and society. But there are also the many bits of folklore attached to divination which tend to lurk in the subconscious. I have lost count of the times I have been asked if it is unlucky to buy your own Tarot cards, or whether using tools of divination will leave you open to dark forces which will take you over. Whilst it is true that a person who is psychologically disturbed could be adversely affected by divination, this could also be said of almost anything; reading fiction, listening to music or eating the wrong food could just as easily be a trigger to a susceptible person. In all honesty, I can say that in my 30 or so years of Craft experience I have only heard one tale of someone having a genuine negative experience, and that case was a small child who was sent to bed early after cutting up an expensive set of Tarot cards!

Lastly, even if you persevere, there are further obstacles. How do you know if you are right about what you perceive, and how do you practise? After all, you don't want to alienate your near and dear by telling them things they would rather you didn't know, nor do you want to look foolish by making predictions which promptly fail. Furthermore, it is notoriously difficult to use divination to answer your own questions, as it is all too easy to give the interpretation which you subconsciously desire, or even dread, to your reading.

Despite all the above, I still find that learning divination is probably the best starting point to accessing the sixth sense, not only for divination itself but also because it gives you the skills to use that sense in other ways. However, I do feel that it is important to choose the system which suits you as an individual.

But what are the divinatory systems? Broadly speaking, you can divide divinatory methods into three groups:

Interpretative – where you actually have images, symbols or numbers, etc, to work with. This group includes the Tarot and other cards, all runes, ogham, tea leaves, and so on. These interpretative methods can be used in intuitive and specific ways; this is one of their strengths. They are also easier for most people to begin with.

Intuitive – where there are no images to work with. These include fire scrying, the dark mirror, crystal ball, etc.

Specific – where you get yes/no answers, like the pendulum, and dowsing or divining rods.

Whilst most of you reading this will be familiar with many forms of divination, here's a quick run down of some of the more commonly used.

Tarot cards: As there are literally hundreds of different Tarot decks, with more coming out all the time, they vary considerably, but basically will have the following structure. A tarot deck will have 78 cards in total, divided into five suits, four of which correspond to the suits in a normal deck of playing cards; these are usually called wands or staves, swords, cups or chalices, and pentacles or coins. These four suits are collectively called the Minor Arcana, and have fourteen cards in each, one more card each than those in playing cards. The fifth suit is called the Major Arcana and takes the form of twenty-two cards, each of which usually has a name and number from 0 to 21. There are two basic types of Tarot deck: fully pictorial where every card has a picture, and semi-pictorial, where the cards of the Minor Arcana are illustrated with an image which simply represents its number, i.e. the five of staves will show five staves. If you are choosing a Tarot deck, I would recommend looking for a fully pictorial one as these are far easier to begin with. I also suggest that you look around for one which you feel some connection with and which is not too expensive. I must confess to some bias here, as the Tarot is one of my preferred methods for divination.

Playing cards: Some people prefer to use ordinary playing cards for divination; of course in this case you will have no pictures to work from, and no fifth suit.

Other decks of cards: There are many other divinatory decks available. If you feel that you would like to work with these, again make a point of looking at several to see which you relate to. Whilst usually fully pictorial, these decks often have far fewer cards than the Tarot and most have no suits, and they also tend to have a single theme, e.g. animals. These can all be limiting factors as they give you less to work from.

Runes: Again, there are a variety of sets of runes around today, so they can vary a lot. Generally speaking, there are 22 runes in a set and they may be made from any of a number of materials including wood, stone, ceramic, etc. Each rune stone has a symbol etched into, or inscribed onto it, although many sets incorporate a blank rune. As mentioned before, the most commonly used runes today are Nordic in origin, although there are others. Each rune equates to a letter but also has a wealth of other meanings associated with it, and their use was originally part of a sophisticated communication system. It is usually recommended that you make your own runes, and then usually at the rate of no more than one a day, or less if you can bear to, as you will need time to meditate on the meanings of each.

Ogham: The Ogham is a system of lines carved into small lengths of wood, called staves. Like the runes, individual characters have a wealth of meaning attached to them. Originally there were 20 but later a further five, the Forfedha, were added making 25 in all.

developing the sixth sense

Witches' Runes: The Witches' Runes are eight stones bearing the following markings: A golden Sun, a silver Moon, two entwined rings, crossed spears, a growing sprig, three birds, a curling wave, and a symbol very similar to #. They are not related to the Nordic, or other, runes in anything other than name.

Tea Leaves: Most people are aware of tea leaf reading as a method of divination, and it does have many advantages. It's cheap; you don't need to lay out much, if any money to try it out. It's socially acceptable virtually everywhere, as very few people object or consider it linked to the devil. The only real drawback is that you do need to learn to drink unstrained tea without swallowing the leaves!

Astrology: The interpretation of planetary positions and movements can be used for divination, in particular to determine the best date(s) for future actions, and to determine potential outcomes of current ones. In the past this would have been quite a lengthy process, but now that there are computer programs which can take out the number crunching it's far more realistic. Having said that, this is really a very minor part of its potential, which can give excellent indicators as to the actions and reactions of individuals on both the broad and, when undertaken by a skilled astrologer, on the specific.

Fire Scrying: Probably one of the earliest forms of divination is looking into the flames and embers of a fire. However, today it is a form which is rarely available to most people. If you wish to experiment with fire, then please ensure that it is safe, not only for yourself, but also for the land, and make sure you have sufficient water to hand to put the flames out thoroughly! Some people find that they can scry in a similar way using a number of candles grouped together.

Dark Mirror: There are two basic forms of dark mirror: solid or liquid. The solid form can be made in several ways. 1: A highly polished piece of black stone such as obsidian, such as was used by the famous Dr John Dee in the sixteenth century, which would probably be prohibitively expensive these days. 2: By layering soot onto the convex surface of a curved glass, usually an old clock face; a fairly messy process involving holding the glass over the flame of a candle or lamp in such a way that the soot is laid down evenly. The non-sooty side is used to look into. 3: By painting the back of either a curved, or more often flat, glass surface with matt black paint and using the other side for scrying. Examples of the latter can be found at many Pagan and Craft stalls these days, often at unwarranted prices. The liquid version is usually created with either water in a dark bowl or basin, or water to which black ink has been added. I have also found that swirling a very little silver ink or powder into the water can help. Either of these is usually positioned so that the light of the Moon, or a candle, is reflected into the surface and this is then used to scry.

Crystal Ball: Crystal balls come in a variety of sizes, from the minuscule to those almost too heavy to lift. These days they can be made from a variety of different kinds of crystal, and hence come in many different colours. But, whilst some Tarot decks and dark mirrors can be expensive, this pales into insignificance compared to the price of a reasonable-sized ball made of crystal! And whilst you can use one made of glass or even lead crystal, which itself is not necessarily cheap, they rarely seem to work so well. Another potential concern about the crystal ball lies in how the crystal was obtained; after all, if you believe in the innate energy of crystals, then you might also like to consider whether those energies may have been affected by being blasted out of the earth, or whether the crystal was gathered in a more sensitive manner.

developing the sixth sense

Pendulum: A pendulum is simply a weight suspended in such a way that it can move freely, although there are many attractive versions available today. The pendulum is used to answer yes/no questions and needs to be 'set' before every use. Setting means determining which movement indicates 'yes' and which indicates 'no' before asking your question(s). Whilst this may sound limiting, it is possible to ask a series of questions in order to determine the answers to quite complex problems. The pendulum can be used for locating things, in a similar way to divining rods, but using maps, rather than outdoors where wind and movement could make it unreliable.

Divining or Dowsing Rods: These are most often used to locate things: water, pipes, mineral deposits, and so on. Their use is not limited to just whether the sought item or substance is present but can be extended to indicate depth and other factors, although like the pendulum, this has to be done using a series of elimination questions. The rods themselves are traditionally created from a forked piece of wood, quite often hazel, which is held lightly and which will move to indicate a positive result. You can also purchase pairs of metal rods which are used together in a similar way. Divining rods can also be used for other yes/no questions.

There are many other forms of divination, and there is certainly not enough room in this book to include them all. Even with the handful I have listed here, I have nowhere near enough space to do them justice. However, I will give some guidelines towards developing the skills of a few, and if you recall the three groups of interpretative, intuitive and specific listed earlier, then you will find that the techniques for one will help you with others in that group. But before we move on to some actual examples and practical work, there are a few things that are worth noting.

The important thing to remember about the tools of divination is that they are just tools. Just as buying a spade will not make your plants flourish unless you learn to use it, purchasing a set of cards, crystal ball, pendulum or whatever will not automatically enable you to access your sixth sense, no matter how much you spend on it.

Give up your misconceptions: many people often talk about 'seeing' when we divine, but this is not to say that pictures appear in front of your eyes nor, most times, even in your head. Whilst a few people actually are clairvoyant, in that they see things in their head, and others are clair-audient, in that they hear the knowledge they divine, by far and away most people find that the knowledge is simply present, with no indication of how it arrived in the mind. Try also to put aside any negative thoughts about divination and the sixth sense which you may have accumulated over time. If it's any help, remember I've been practising for thirty years with no ill effects, or at least thus far!

Be patient and honest with yourself; just like any other form of magical practice you won't be at your best if tired, worried or ailing. So try to take it a little at a time. Keep coming back to it, but don't overdo it and definitely don't try to push it; remember, the harder you chase something, the harder it will run away.

But most of all, learn to trust your instincts. Many years ago someone came to me for a reading and asked me to perform psychometry on a piece of her grandmother's jewellery. On reaching out for the piece I had a flash of 'knowing' and without even thinking said, 'You don't want to know about your grandmother, you want to know if your boyfriend's faithful'. Now if I had stopped to consider, I almost certainly wouldn't have said that, partly because people rarely want information they haven't asked for, but also because my mind wasn't even slightly focused in that direction. But I was right, and that hasn't been the only time when knowledge has not only come out of nowhere, but has also been unsought. Of course, you can't go through

developing the sixth sense

life blurting out unsupported nuggets of information at all and sundry, especially when they're not looking for the information. What you can do, however, is use your journal, or a separate one, as a place to make notes and to refer back to at a later point. In fact, you may find it helpful to keep a small notebook with you at all times for this purpose, and that way you won't have to remember things to write up later. For, once you start working with your sixth sense, you will find that insights do not always wait for you to seek them.

PRACTICAL WORK 1

If you haven't already done so, take some stiff card and cut it into twelve pieces of exactly the same shape and about the size of playing cards. Colour each on one side only, which we'll call the face, in one each of the following colours: brown, red, orange, yellow, green, blue, indigo, violet, black, white, gold and silver. Make sure that there is no way of seeing from the uncoloured side what colour the face is.

Shuffle the cards and spread them face down in front of you. Close your eyes, take a few deep breaths, and choose a colour. When you start out it is best to select a colour with which you have a strong affinity. Then, hold your strong hand palm down over each in turn, and see if you can detect which is the colour you seek. You may find it easier if you touch your fingertips to each card in turn, and you may also want to go backwards and forwards over the cards several times. When you think you can detect the colour you seek, turn the card over and see if you were right or not. If your first try is wrong, keep going until you locate the colour you seek. Try this with each of the colours in turn, shuffling the cards each time and making notes on each; you may be surprised at which colour(s) you have an affinity with.

Needless to say, the odds are against you getting it right first time, so don't be too disappointed if you don't pick the right one immediately. But this will give you a benchmark before going onto other practical work, perhaps using tools which you have some knowledge of, or may already have worked with.

developing the sixth sense

There are many uses for divination: to answer specific questions, to seek general guidance for the future and to understand more about the past and present. However, whether or not you intend to use it for the above, divination is also an excellent way of exercising the sixth sense. The following three pieces of practical work relate to the three basic groups of divination techniques. For ease of reference I have chosen to talk about one divinatory method from each group, but you could substitute any other from the same group if you prefer. If you are interested in learning divination for its own sake, then you may find it helpful to try several methods to see which suits you best.

PRACTICAL WORK 2
— INTERPRETATIVE DIVINATIONS

My preferred method of interpretative divination is the Tarot. Whilst I have used other methods, it's the one I find easiest and the one with which I get the most accurate and consistent results. As I said earlier, the best type of deck to start with is the fully pictorial, and the most commonly used of these is the Rider Waite deck. If your deck has a booklet, set this aside for now. If you want to read it for interest later, fine, but don't try to learn the interpretations it contains. One of the reasons for this is that these will be the thoughts and feelings of the author, not your own, and, after all, it is you, not they, who will be using the cards!

Take out the cards and have a look through them. Consider each in turn, and think about your immediate impression: Does the card give you a positive or negative feeling? Do you feel it looks forward or refers to the past?

Look at the four suits in the Minor Arcana, bearing in mind that they link to the Elements; wands or staves to Air, swords to Fire, cups to Water and coins or pentacles to Earth. If looked at in sequence, does there seem to be a story or thread running through the suit, or a common theme? There may not be, as some decks are not constructed this way. Are there similarities between the same card from different suits, for example do all the five's show conflict?

Look separately at the Major Arcana; again is there a story or thread which runs through the suit? The Major Arcana is linked to the Element of Spirit, and in many decks shows the stages of development of the individual. If you feel this applies to yours, which stage do you feel marks your life at present?

Once you have a basic familiarity with the deck, shuffle the cards well. Some Tarot readers recommend that you place the deck under your pillow, or beside the bed, for a few nights, to strengthen your link with your cards. But you may find the following more useful.

In the evening, shuffle your cards whilst thinking about the day to come, then lay out three cards face down. As you do so, name the first 'morning', the second 'afternoon', and the last 'evening'. Put the other cards to one side. Turn over your first card and study it carefully. Look at the picture as though at a photograph. Ask yourself what is happening, what happened before the image and what may happen next. If there are people, who are they and what are their lives like? Note also the detail in the background of the image: what do the component parts mean to you? Now consider your thoughts, feelings and impressions in association with your own life, in particular the coming morning. What do you feel that the card indicates in your life? It is important to be aware of both your immediate impression and those impressions you gain after studying the picture. Make notes on all these aspects, and then repeat the process with the cards for afternoon and then evening. Put these aside for review later.

If you are new to the Tarot this may be the moment to explain that the imagery in the cards is rarely to be taken literally. The card Death, for example, usually indicates a major change, perhaps the 'death' of a phase or aspect of life; it most certainly does not mean you are going to drop dead in the morning!

the real witches' craft

The following evening, take out your notes and review them in the light of the events of the morning, afternoon and evening respectively. Compare the events of your day with the cards, and with the thoughts and feelings you noted down. Repeat this exercise two or three times a week, or daily if you feel able. Most probably you will find that you draw different cards most times. But if you find the same cards coming up very frequently, despite shuffling them well, then you may want to meditate on the meaning of those cards.

It will take time, but you will soon find yourself developing a good working understanding of your cards, as well as your own way of interpreting them. Once you are familiar with the cards you can move onto doing more complex readings; there should be at least one layout described in the booklet you put to one side at the beginning.

developing the sixth sense

PRACTICAL WORK 3
— SPECIFIC DIVINATIONS

For this group I have selected the pendulum, partly because it is my preferred method here, but also because it is simple to make one if you want to. Take a relatively heavy object and suspend it from a thread: a pebble with a hole in is ideal, or you could use one of those crystals which are sold to hang in the window to catch the light.

As mentioned above, a pendulum needs to be set before each session of use. Hold the thread in your strong hand, the right if you are right handed, over the palm of the other hand, in such a way that it can move freely. Close your eyes and think the strongest 'no' you can, the sort of no you would shout if someone you loved were about to be harmed. Hold this thought for a few seconds whilst trying not to move the hand holding the thread. Open your eyes and carefully observe the movement of the pendulum; swinging backwards and forwards, circling or whatever. Now repeat these actions, thinking the strongest 'yes' that you can. You will now have two distinct movements to work with.

Formulate your question with care, so that it can be answered with yes or no. Once again, hold the pendulum in the same way, close your eyes and ask it. The reason for closing your eyes is to help you to avoid influencing the pendulum's movement in favour of the answer you consciously, or subconsciously, wish for. After a few moments, open your eyes and see whether your answer is yes or no. Sometimes the pendulum may move in a way which is not the same as your yes or no directions, or it may not move at all. If this happens, relax yourself and then ask the question again. If you still have an ambiguous movement, then it could be that your question was not clear enough, or that you are not meant to know. Alternatively, it can indicate that the answer is 'maybe' and that the outcome is within your ability to create. For example, if your question was, 'Will I speak to my sister?' this question is unclear because you have not specified when, and the outcome is also within your influence because you could contact her.

If you are asking a series of questions in one session, related to a single topic, then you do not have to reset the pendulum between each question. But if you change topic, or take a break between questions then you should reset it.

developing the sixth sense

PRACTICAL WORK 4
— INTUITIVE DIVINATIONS

I have left intuitive divination until last because it is, for most people, the hardest skill to acquire, and is usually best practised after you have worked on at least one of the methods from the other two groups first.

In this group I have chosen the liquid dark mirror, as it is a relatively easy one to create. Take a bowl or dish with a diameter of around nine or more inches, fill it with water and place it in such a way that the light of the full Moon or of a candle will reflect in its surface. Do this before adding anything to the water, to minimize the risk of messy spills. Add some black ink until the water appears black and reflective, and then add one or two drops of silver ink to the centre of the bowl and stir them lightly so that they lie on the surface, rather than being mixed in.

Settle yourself comfortably, in a seated position, so that you can see the reflection of the Moon or candle in the water, and take several deep breaths to relax yourself. Formulate your question in your mind and gaze, rather than stare, into the water. Let your inner sight descend into, and merge with, the water. You are not looking for images, but rather waiting for impressions to be felt within. Some people find they have a falling sensation as though they are separating from their body and falling into the water.

The first few times you do this you may feel that nothing is happening, but do persevere as it often takes several sessions before you are able to relax your mind sufficiently for you to be able to gather any impressions. It's definitely a case of the harder you try, the less easily it comes! Some people find that it is helpful to have an inspirational incense burning nearby to help them to relax their conscious mind.

Divination is like any other skill; the more you practise the better you will become. But having said that, if you use it for frivolous purposes then you may find that your ability wanes. This is not some form of divine retribution but the simple fact that your inner mind will know that you are misusing your ability and simply stop co-operating. However, this does not prevent you practising, so long as you are genuinely seeking knowledge.

Finding a Good Reader

I said earlier that it is difficult to do your own readings, yet this varies considerably from person to person and also according to your need to have the question answered. The more weight you place on having an answer, the more likely you will interpret your reading according to your own desires. Given the difficulty of doing your own readings, I am often asked how to find a good reader to do divination for you.

Regrettably, there are people who range from those who are either just not very good, to those who are definitely charlatans preying on the gullible. The following should help you to avoid some of the problem areas.

A good reader will state clearly what, if anything, they charge, and rarely ask for payment 'up front'. Moreover, their charges will be reasonable; those expensive telephone lines could be manned by anybody.

developing the sixth sense

Good readers rarely have to take out expensive and regular advertisements, as reputation usually gets them all the business they can handle. They tend to look and behave like 'normal' people, without a lot of scenic trappings and atmospherics. They will either allow you to take notes or possibly offer you a recording of your reading. They will certainly not suggest that you must come back for further readings on a frequent basis.

Probably the simplest solution is to go to someone who has been personally recommended by a person whose judgement you trust.

Other Uses for the Sixth Sense

Of course the sixth sense is not limited to divination; it can be used to sense many other things, for example, energy fields, such as those associated with ley lines and places of power like ancient worship and burial sites. It can detect residual energies which can be found in homes and other buildings, often in places where there have been strong emotions these are sometimes considered to be a form of 'ghost'. It can help you to sense spiritual energies, including the presence of others who may seek to overlook you; personal energies such as auras; and, of course, places of magical working, such as those frequently used for Rituals. In short, the sixth sense can detect a whole range of energies which are not usually noticed by the other five senses.

As you work on developing your sixth sense you may begin to become aware of some of these energies around you from time to time. These are not usually harmful or threatening in any way; most are simply present, just as background noise is present. Should you find yourself visiting a place where you sense something, you can choose to either seek to learn more or, if it feels uncomfortable, to walk away. Personally, I have a great deal of curiosity and tend, on the whole, to want to find out more and, after protecting myself with a Circle, will open my mind to any impressions. To protect yourself, mentally

the real witches' craft

invoke each of the Elements, call upon the Goddess and the God, and cast the Circle so that it envelops you. If you have someone with you, expand the Circle to include them too. It's also really not fair to encourage external energies if you are with someone who is very young, unwell or liable to be adversely affected by the experience. It's much better to come back on your own at a later date.

However, energies in the home can sometimes be irritating, or can result in physical manifestations which are inconvenient. I lived for a while in a house where there was a 'presence' which left pins behind. At the time this was not a problem, I simply had to remember not to walk barefoot in that room! But that was before I had a child. Were I to live there now then I would probably need to tackle the problem. Negative energies left behind by previous occupants can also be annoying, especially when they affect the moods and emotions of those you live with. A house which has seen a lot of argument or unhappiness can lead to those feelings being more common in the new occupants than they otherwise would be. Of course, most Witches ritually cleanse and protect their home fairly regularly as well as when they move in, and this is usually enough to rid it of negative influences as well as protect it, and you, from energies trying to gain entrance. I'd like to point out that it is very rare for anyone to be the target of negative magic or psychic attack, despite folk-myths to the contrary. However, we will visit these in more detail in the last chapter of this book.

'Controlling' your Sixth Sense

Just like any other skill or talent, the ability to use your sixth sense varies from person to person. Some people will find it easy to access, others will need to practise regularly, and some may find that they are only rarely able to use it. However, for a few, the difficulty lies not in getting in touch with their sixth sense, but in how to turn it off. If you are having difficulty using your sixth sense you may have little sympathy with the idea of wanting not

developing the sixth sense

to use it, but it can be miserable to be assailed by unexpected and unwanted psychic energies. And, as there can be times when even the least sensitive may find this happening, it is a good idea for everyone to learn how to 'shut down'. It can also be a useful technique to use if you find yourself in the company of people who are psychically draining, sometimes called psychic vampires.

PRACTICAL WORK 5
— THE INNER CIRCLE

Invoke the Elements, invite the Goddess and the God and cast the Circle, all in your mind. Visualize the Circle enveloping you and you alone. Now visualize it shrinking and moving in through your skin so that it forms a layer just under the surface of your whole body. Ask the Goddess and the God to protect you and to strengthen this, your Inner Circle. Visualize the Inner Circle being flecked with small grains of silver, the number increasing until the whole is a silver barrier protecting you. When it is in place, thank the Goddess and the God and the Elements, but do not banish them. Once you have this in place, do not attempt any psychic or magical work, as doing so will breach your protection and will also affect your working.

Retain the Circle within for as long as you feel you need it. To remove it, visualize the shield beneath your skin, then visualize the silver breaking up and once again turning into flecks of light. Once these have all dissipated and you have only the electric blue of your normal Circle, you can expand it until it is outside your body and then banish it in the normal way.

If you are psychically sensitive, you may want to leave the protection in place at all times, other than for magical workings. In this case, you would cast your Circle in the usual way, before expanding and removing the protective one. Similarly, after working, replace the protection before removing your

developing the sixth sense

usual Circle. This form of protection should be renewed at every full Moon to keep it in good working order.

Many people, whatever their level or experience, have difficulties with accessing and using their sixth sense from time to time. This fluctuation is often linked to the cycle of the Moon. Although it is sometimes said that certain phases are better for psychic work than others, this can vary from person to person. So when you make your notes, be sure to include the Moon's phase, and as much other detail as you can, to help you to determine the best times for you as an individual.

The best way to develop your sixth sense is through regular practise and learning to trust in your insights. When using it in a formal manner, perhaps when doing a reading, you may also find it helps to burn candles or incense, and to wear, or have by you, crystals and gemstones. These work in much the same way as other types of magical aids: they provide visual and tactile links and may contribute to your working, but they will not do the work for you. Having said that, if you find it helpful to use some form of amulet or talisman, then by all means do so.

RITUAL TO CONSECRATE
TOOLS OF DIVINATION

Once you have selected your preferred tool or tools of divination, they can be empowered and consecrated. For the three nights prior to the full Moon, place it, or them, in the light of the Moon: an inside windowsill is best.

At the full Moon lay your Altar, including salt crystals, water, burning incense and a lighted candle. Invoke the Elements, invite the Goddess and the God and cast your Circle in your usual way. Begin by asking the Goddess and the God to give you insight and understanding, ask them to guide your inner sight and to give you the wisdom to know. Settle yourself down and place your divination tool(s) in front of you. If this is a set, such as cards or runes, then spread them out, handle and look at each in turn. If it is a single item then simply handle it, whilst letting your mind get to know its form. Don't try to scry at this time, just to understand the inner nature of your tool(s). When you feel that you have made a connection with the tools, move on to consecrating them. Hold the tool(s) in your receiving hand (the left if you are left handed, or vice versa), then pass them through the incense smoke, visualizing the Element of Air and thought entering them. Pass them over the candle flame (being careful not to burn your hand) visualizing the Element of Fire and passion imbuing them. Sprinkle a few drops of water onto them whilst visualizing Water and emotion, and lastly sprinkle a little salt onto them whilst visualizing Earth and the physical realm. Hold them in both hands and call upon the Goddess and the God to bless them.

Once you have finished the consecration, dismiss the Elements, thank the Goddess and the God and close your Circle in your usual way.

developing the sixth sense

After consecration, wrap your divination tool in a violet or purple cloth, or one of your preferred colour, or place it in a pouch of the same colour. This should be made of a natural, not man-made, fabric. Include with your tool a small sprig of Broom, some Witch-grass or an ear of Corn. Tie the whole together with a silver cord. From this point onwards, do not allow others to handle your tools, unless it is during the course of a reading.

If you wish, you can also consecrate a special crystal to keep with your divination tools. There are many to choose from but a clear quartz crystal point, or a piece of natural flint, are both excellent choices as they help to open the pathways through which psychic energies can pass. You might also like to wear a similar stone when scrying. If you have difficulty with being too receptive to psychic energy, then wear a smoky quartz or a holed stone.

In addition to using divination to check the potential outcome(s) of a spell, you can also use it to see whether the spell is actually necessary. Quite often, a problem will in fact resolve itself in a satisfactory way without magical intervention. If you look forward, to see what is going to happen without a spell, you may find that the outcome you seek is already in progress.

Some of the tools of divination are also used to actually cast spells. The Tarot and the runes are the most well known for this. The technique involves selecting the cards, or whatever, which you consider embody the spirit or essence of your spell. Usually this will be a number between three and seven, to cover the necessary steps. Empower them within the Circle and set them aside until the spell takes effect. The obvious drawback is that this then leaves your tool of divination depleted until the spell has run its course.

But magic is, as I have said before, not about the tools of divination, nor even of the Craft itself.

the real witches' craft

Chapter Seven

CRAFTING SPELLS:

The Basis of Magic

Magic is inextricably linked to the Craft, from the small spells we work to help us in daily life to the larger ones which may be directed at the land. For most Witches the practice of magic is a key part of their Craft; indeed for some it was this which led them to choose it as their path. But whilst we know magic can work, sometimes our spells do not give the results we hope for or expect.

To understand why this is, we need to look at some of the basic tenets of magic. Whilst we say, understandably with some pride, that the Craft does not have a long list of prohibitions, there are nevertheless a number of 'rules' or principles which govern the use of magic. These are not rules in the same way that a country has laws, designed to provide curbs on the impulses of the anti-social, but more in the way of laws of nature; rules, which if not followed, can make your magic unreliable or less effective. Although you may be familiar with some of these it is still a good idea to revisit them, just as it can be with many of the things you learned at the outset of your magical studies. As you grow in your Craft your perception and understanding also grow, and when you take the time to look at some of the things you learned in the early days you may well find that you have a new and deeper appreciation of them now.

The Wiccan Rede: 'An it harm none, do what you will,' is probably the most often quoted principle of the Craft. Whilst at first sight this seems simply to say that Magic should not be used to harm, it does have a second and equally important message; it is the application of your will which makes magic work. This has to be your true will, not just an idle thought or wish. Think of this as being a difference in effort similar to that between pushing a heavy object on well-oiled wheels or one which is flat on soggy ground. The 'An it harm none' part is subject to quite a lot of discussion, partly as it is virtually impossible to do anything which does not harm someone or something, after all even our very existence on the planet does harm to many things. However, the most usually accepted interpretation is to do no deliberate harm, or that which would be avoidable by carefully considering the consequences. Having said that, I cannot answer for you, but I would feel responsible if my magic caused harm, whether or not I had envisaged the result. Some versions of the Rede go on to add, 'lest in thine own defence it be, and ever mind the rule of three.' Certainly the Rede would not prevent me from practising defensive magic, whether on my own behalf or for someone else, just as I would feel little sympathy if a burglar hurt themselves climbing over my fine and very thorny hedge!

The Law of Three-fold Return, or the 'Rule of Three' referred to above, states: 'Whatever you do, good or ill, will be returned to you three times over'. A well-respected elder of the Craft once stated that she was not happy with this as she did not believe that Witches were singled out for some kind of divine retribution. I would agree that the Law of Three-fold Return is not aimed specifically at Witches or their Magic, but I do believe in a similar concept of

the real witches' craft

'what goes around, comes around.' In other words, if you do good things, good things will happen to you, and vice versa. Interestingly, when I worked in a shop we had a charity box which rarely received any donations, so I put a copy of the law of Three-fold Return on its side, and lo and behold contributions soared, even though very few of the visitors were actually Witches. Obviously, the concept rings true in the psyche, whatever your beliefs. The Law of Three-fold Return is almost certainly an import from eastern mysticism, and is quite unnecessary if you are already trying to follow the Rede.

The Magical, or Magician's, Rules: 'To know, to will, to dare, and to keep silent.'

> **To Know** – simply means you need knowledge to work magic; not only the technical knowledge of how to make a spell, but also the true knowledge that it will work. If you have any doubts, these will prevent you from making the magic work. Interestingly, magic works because the practitioner believes in it, regardless of whether the recipient believes, although should they actively disbelieve then the energy of that disbelief may effect it.

> **To Will** – means that you need to truly will it (as mentioned in the Rede); you must want it to work with every fibre of your being. Again, if you have any doubts about its 'rightness' these will interfere with your magic; in fact if you have any doubts at all then don't do it.

> **To Dare** – you need to actually do it; even though I have said that spells sometimes start to work once you have designed them, they will not be at 'full power' unless you actually do it!

crafting spells: the basis of magic

To Keep Silent – you should keep your own counsel about your spells. It is this latter aspect which confuses some people, after all, if you worked in a group everyone there would have to know what spell they were working. Probably the easiest way to illustrate the need for silence is to think of it this way: when you are angry or really upset you have very strong feelings, but after you discuss these with a close friend you begin to feel better and the feelings dissipate. Magical energy can also drain away in a similar manner. Moreover, the more people who know about an intended act of magic, the more likely that one of them may have doubts about it, and those doubts can produce their own energy which may affect the result, or dilute the energy, of your spell. This is why in a group it is essential that everyone agrees with the magic to be worked. Even after a spell has been performed, it is better to say nothing.

Other factors which have impact on the working of magic:

A spell should not interfere with another person's freedom of will, e.g. any form of magic which would make one person fall in love with another. However, this also includes not working spells which might appear beneficial, for example to make someone stop smoking. Although there is no doubt that this would be a good thing, you still should not do it without their consent. One way round this would be to create a form of spell which they can choose to use or not; an empowered candle or talisman perhaps.

Spells should not be worked to directly obtain money. No doubt you have heard this before and the reasons why, but it does no harm to repeat that money spells are invariably bad news! Because money is not a part of the natural world this can result in many kinds of difficulty, e.g. you work a spell for money, your car is then involved in an accident which you can claim for on the insurance. Yes, you have gained some money, but you have also

gained another need to spend it, and possibly some injuries as well. Far better to work a spell for the opportunity to earn money, or for a promotion.

Magic should not be performed for payment, although it is acceptable to cover your costs. Certainly, if you are empowering a piece of jewellery for someone, you can expect them to provide the jewellery or to pay for it. Having said that, if you are asking someone to expend time and effort on your behalf it is only good manners to give them something in return, a small gift, perhaps. The difference lies between someone demanding payment for magic and you voluntarily showing your appreciation for someone's time and energy.

Spells should not be worked to impress, as a joke or without good reason. If you waste your magical resources on frivolous spells, those resources will not be so readily available when you really need them. Should you want to practise a new magical technique and can really not think of a suitable cause, then consider working for the land or wildlife in general.

Magic works through the exchange of energies; the more energy you put into your spell, the more effective it will be.

Magic rarely works instantly; it usually takes time for a spell to come to fruition. Generally speaking, the more complex the problem, or the spell, the longer it will take. Sometimes a spell which you perform regularly will be more rapid in effect.

As magic needs your energy, it will not work well if you are out of balance. This may mean that you cannot work healing spells if you are very ill, but it is far better to wait rather than to risk your magic going wrong.

Spells do not have to be put into rhyme for them to work. If you are poetic, or prefer rhyming incantations, then by all means use them, but they are not essential. From time to time you may come across spells or incantations with words which you do not understand, in which case don't use them. If you don't know what the words mean, you can't be certain what you are asking for.

Magic does not need special clothes, tools, etc to work. However, if you find that these things make it easier to focus, as they often can be, or that they give more comfort to the person you are working for, then by all means use them. I shall be looking at some of the ways of focusing magic in the next chapter.

But even if we take all the above into account, our spells and magic may not work out as we expect. Probably the most common reason for this is a lack of foresight. If you don't plan your magic carefully, then you won't get the result you seek. An oft told, and possibly apocryphal, tale is told where someone worked magic for gold and received golden flowers, a goldfish and a small, admittedly shiny, coin. Furthermore, it is possible to set into action a chain of events which, whilst intended to bring about one result, may actually produce a different one. These are just a couple of the reasons why the most important part of working magic lies in the planning.

Most of the time when you feel you have cause to craft a spell, it is better to give it careful thought rather than to spring into immediate action. Obviously, some matters are urgent, but it is important to recognize that these are actually extremely rare. As I write I find it quite hard to think of an example which would not benefit from even just ten minutes of careful thought before setting off to work a spell. But if you find yourself in any doubt you have only to ask yourself the question: what is the worst that will happen if I stop and think, and will that be worse than getting it wrong?

There is, however, a series of fairly straightforward steps which can be taken to help towards successful spells:

- ❀ Identify the problem;
- ❀ Look for any underlying causes;
- ❀ Determine whether magical intervention is really the answer;
- ❀ Design the spell;
- ❀ Check for potential results and side effects;
- ❀ Perform the spell.

When considering a spell, start by looking carefully at the problem and its causes. Very few things in life are as straightforward as they first appear, so try to look at it from different perspectives. This is particularly important when it comes to any kind of relationship difficulty, as rarely will you be able to fully appreciate both sides of the tale. A careful look at the causes of a problem can often give you a better idea of what form of spell to create. For example, if the problem is, so to speak, too much month left at the end of the money, then the cause could be a tendency to shop for clothes to boost low self-esteem. In this case, the simplest solution is to raise the person's self-confidence, rather than working to get them a higher paid and more responsible job which could result in greater, not less, anxiety and loss of self-esteem leading to the desire to spend even more to make up for it.

crafting spells: the basis of magic

PRACTICAL WORK 1

Take a look at a television programme involving people and their problems; soap operas are the most obvious example. Choose one of the more problematic characters and look to see if you can identify the root cause(s) of their problems. Try this first after watching only one or two episodes. Then review your analysis after several more. You'll find that the more you see of the character the greater your understanding will be.

By the way, I've chosen to use TV rather than the real world as these characters are fictional and therefore their problems are usually rather more black and white than those in the real world. If you don't watch TV then you could do the same with a character from a book, although this can be somewhat harder.

From this you will see that a perceived problem can often be the symptom of a deeper issue, and it will be more successful in the long term to address the cause rather than the symptoms. You may have thought from your reading of spell books that there is a specific solution to every small glitch or problem encountered in daily life, but quite often our problems are rooted in issues which come up over and over again. Having said that, unless you are qualified, you shouldn't try to psychoanalyse other people, nor should you be trying to treat any problems in the usual sense. It is one thing to feel that there is an underlying problem, and quite another to try to get someone to confront it. This may seem like a contradiction, but it is really just a matter of degree. A person's love of shopping may be a symptom of their underlying insecurity, and it is fine to address this by giving them more self-confidence, rather than working for increased income. It is not, however, a good idea to go rooting around in someone's psyche to see what caused this lack in the first place, unless specifically asked to. Of course, in addition to thinking through the causes of a problem, we can also use our skills of meditation and divination to help identify the underlying cause.

PRACTICAL WORK 2

Use the same storyline as for the previous exercise, and first perform a meditation on the problem concerned. When you have finished, make notes on any impressions you have gained. Secondly, take your preferred method of divination and see if you can use it to give you further information on the causes of the problem.

At this point, it is worth recalling that not every difficulty in life is best solved using magic alone, or even by using magic at all. Say, for example, your best friend's partner has left them and they are understandably really upset. This is probably the occasion to go around with a box of tissues and a bottle of wine, rather than casting a spell. Grief in particular is often best left to run its course. This may seem harsh but even at times of bereavement it is often better to allow the natural process to take its course, rather than to intervene directly. Of course, you may decide that whilst the main problem will not benefit from magical attention, there are side issues which you can help with. Using our example of bereavement; whilst it may be best to let the grief run its natural course, you could work to give them restful and healing sleep, or strength to carry on with daily life. To give another example: If I am struggling with a book (as can happen occasionally!), then a spell to enable me to write the 'right' words would not really be an option. You cannot magically write for me. But a spot of practical help to take care of other day-to-day chores and distractions would free me up to be creative. And a spell to bring me inspiration and concentration would also be useful.

There is one particular kind of occasion when you should not work magic, and that is for revenge. Even if you, or someone you love, have been seriously hurt, do not work a spell for revenge, or when you are feeling vengeful. The old saying that revenge is a dish best eaten cold is true, and more often than not there are better ways of ensuring that a person gets what is coming to them, but more of this later in the book.

So the next step we need to consider is whether the best thing is to work magic or not, and if so what kind. This can be broken down into two questions; what will happen if you do nothing, and what may happen if you work a particular spell. To answer the first you can use divination and meditation. But to answer the second you need to have some idea of what sort of spell, or spells, you might want to work.

crafting spells: the basis of magic

PRACTICAL WORK 3

Again, using your TV character and their current scenario, give some thought as to whether magic would be helpful or not. Would it be best to direct a spell at the main cause of their problem, or are there other aspects of their life which could be enhanced to help them through this time? With a little thought you should be able to come up with a selection of possible spells. As this is just an exercise, try to limit yourself to three options: one to do nothing, a spell to directly affect the main issue and a different spell to enhance their own ability to solve the problem. For each of the three options, perform both a meditation and a divination to see if you can determine the potential outcome of each course of action. It's best to take a break between each of the three, perhaps stopping for a coffee or the like, before moving on to the next, so that you can clear your mind for each.

Of course, when it comes to deciding what sort of spells to work for real people you may come up with more or fewer options. In some cases the solution may seem obvious, whereas in others you may want to use the above technique to select from a number of options. Remember, as with all your exercises, to make notes in your journal. I realize that I stress this a lot, but it's surprising how useful it can be as your magic progresses to be able to refer back to the things you did along the way.

This whole process for deciding what to work may sound lengthy, as indeed it is when you first start using it. But with a little practice these steps become second nature and will only take a short while. It's important to remember that effective magic is not a quick fix; the more planning and thought you put into it at the beginning, the more likely it is that your spells will bring the results you want. In the following chapter I shall be looking at some of the techniques you can use to work your spells as well as ways of crafting them. But before moving on to that, there are a couple more points about effective magic that I'd like to cover.

The term 'Rule of Three' mentioned above is also thought to refer to another aspect of magical practice; that of crafting spells in threes. To understand why, we need to remember that the Craft is not just about magic, it is a spiritual path in its own right. It is often referred to as a nature based belief system, and this reminds us that we are a part of the cycles of the seasons and the land, and that we seek balance in our lives and in our relationship with the world. So perhaps it is not surprising that our magical work should reflect this; when we work we perform one spell for ourselves, one for someone else and one for nature and/or the land, bringing us back into balance with the world we live in.

This three-fold spell-craft may not be practical every time you are working, especially if you are magically busy, but it is certainly something you should consider doing at least once a month, perhaps as a part of your Esbat rites. Performing a spell for the land reinforces our relationship with nature and allows us to give something back. This spell should be something which benefits nature in some way; perhaps towards protecting an endangered species, or for local wildlife, or even to encourage drivers to avoid animals on the roads. Performing a spell for another ensures that our magic does not become self-centred, which can happen at times of stress. And remembering to perform a spell for yourself prevents the opposite problem; that of forgetting to use magic for self help. A surprising number of practising Witches frequently omit to work magic on their own behalf. I've lost count of the times someone has come to me for help and when asked what spells they have worked reply, none.

PRACTICAL WORK 4

Prepare for your next full Moon ritual by working on three spells using the above technique. As I appreciate that sometimes inspiration can fail, here are just a few ideas:

For yourself: Increased psychic ability. To find a magical friend or mentor. Greater patience with those close to you.

For someone you know: Healing of a physical injury. Increased self-confidence. More time for relaxation.

For the nature and the land: Preservation of the natural habitat of an endangered species, locally or internationally. The protection of a particular species; in my area a lot of hares get run over because they dance on the roads on moonlit nights. A good harvest.

Consider the problem, the cause, whether magic will help, what type of spell, the potential outcomes, side effects, and so on. Make notes in advance of your working, so that later you can compare what actually happened with your intent.

Sometimes we prepare for a particular spell or spells only to find that by the time of the working something more pressing has come up. When this happens, by all means substitute the more pressing spell for one which can wait, but still give some time to considering all the factors as before. We all

the real witches' craft

have times when it seems as though the magical work is backing up and there are a great number of spells waiting for our attention. In these cases it is best to stick to the most urgent, rather than to try to do everything at one time. Your inner Magical resources are finite, and your energy is limited. You should notice that after a strong working you are physically and mentally tired. If you try to do too many things at one time, you will not be able to give sufficient energy to any of them. If you really do have a number of pressing spells at any one time, then you will need to prioritize them. Don't try to work more than three on any one day, and don't work for more than three consecutive days. If, at any point, you feel you are not giving your best, then stop work for that day and see how you feel on the following one. Remember, you want to work effective magic. And don't be afraid to ask for help from other Witches, either those you know or via a good website on the internet.

Furthermore, the bigger the spell, the more magic is required. My spell to protect hares in my locality will have some effect after just the one working. But were I to try to protect all hares, I would need either to repeat the spell regularly or to get others to join with me in the spell. If I wanted to go further and wish to protect all wildlife everywhere, then the chances of my magic being completely successful are remote, but every spell I work towards the intended result will have some positive effect. Whilst this may be frustrating, it's a good thing; the world would be a terrifying place if just one spell by just one Witch could make a huge impact! Generally speaking, your magic will work most effectively on things which are close to you, both geographically and emotionally. Hence remote working for your Aunt is more likely to be effective than for a stranger. But were the stranger close by, and you had strong links to them, for example their picture and date of birth, then your chances of helping them are increased. One of the potentially disappointing aspects of working spells is that quite often we don't know whether our magic is working or not. But that doesn't mean it is not worth working. I may not know which hares I keep out of the way of traffic; but I do know that, if well crafted, my spell will help some.

THREE-FOLD MAGIC RITUAL

Take your prepared spells from 'Practical Work 4' above and, making sure that you have all the equipment you need, create your Sacred Space in your usual way.

Begin by performing the spell you feel strongest about, as this is the one which is uppermost in your mind. Once this is out of the way, so to speak, you will be better able to focus on the next, and so on. As you are doing a sequence of spells, which may not be linked to one another, you'll need to have a clear break between each one and the next, and to raise energy for each independently. So your sequence should go like this: raise energy, spell, raise energy, spell, raise energy, spell. If you are creating or blessing objects, such as a talisman or amulet, it is a good idea to have a cloth to wrap each in, and to be able to put it to the side of the Altar before moving on to the next spell. Likewise, candles can be placed to the back of the Altar, keeping the centre for working the current spell.

When you have completed all three spells, clear away in the usual manner, placing candles or objects carefully to one side, and write it up as usual.

I have briefly mentioned talismans and amulets, but there are a great many ways of working magic, some of which you'll find in the following chapter.

the real witches' craft

Chapter Eight

MAGICAL METHODS

Whilst it is perfectly possible to work spells and magic entirely on the astral or psychic plane, with no tools and equipment whatsoever, most of us find it easier to use some, at least some of the time. They help us to focus on the purpose of the spell, and its subject. They enable us to create a spell which can be activated by another, at the time they think is right. They remind us of the basic aspects of the Craft and their place in our magic.

They also serve to help create the atmosphere and environment which make it easier to summon our magical intent, energy, focus and strength. When more than one person is working they also serve to keep everyone focused on the same thing at the same time. But having said that, very, very few of them are actually essential. If you feel you can work without them then do so, but if, like me, you like to make your magic easier from time to time, then use the ones which you find useful.

Generally speaking, magical tools and equipment fall into three distinct groupings:

- *Tools of the Craft* – those considered part of the Altar and working equipment, including those used to create the Sacred Space.
- *Links to the subject* – these provide you with a greater connection to the person or subject you are working for. They may include a photograph, picture, description, personal information, or even hair and nail clippings.
- *Magical methods* – the tools: candles, cords, amulets, talismans, etc, through which the magic is made to work, and the ways of using them.

For the sake of completeness I will run through all three groupings in this chapter, although by this point in your studies you will almost certainly be very familiar with those in the first category. Those in the second two categories I shall talk about in more detail as these are the magical methods of the chapter title. You may have already worked with some, others may be unfamiliar, or you may not have considered them for a long time. Many practising Witches find that they get into a sort of magical rut, working the same spells and using the same techniques, with the appropriate alterations, for almost every act of magic. This is understandable; you develop preferences for particular types of spell either because they are tried and trusted, or perhaps because the method fits conveniently into your life. However, sometimes we can become a bit blinkered and forget to consider whether there are any alternatives.

The Tools of the Craft

As this book is intended for Witches who have already been practising a while, I will give only a brief description of these. If you'd like more information then it can be found in *The Real Witches' Handbook* and others.

- ❈ *Altar* – The surface on which you place any other tools or equipment, and the area on which you work. Unless you are working entirely on the Astral you will need some kind of surface, even if it is only a cleared space on the floor.

- ❈ *Altar cloth* – A cloth which covers the Altar to define its use in a magical context and to protect the surface from wax spills and the like.

- ❈ *Altar pentagram* – A flat board or stone with the five-pointed star within a circle inscribed upon it. This forms the working surface for spell craft, and if you are doing anything tangible then it's a good firm surface to work on.

- ❈ *Element symbols* – to represent the Elements of Air, Fire, Water, Earth and Spirit. Incense in a heatproof container for Air. A lighted candle for Fire. A dish of water for Water. Salt in a container for Earth. These are not usually necessary when working outside, as the elements are truly present!

- ❈ *Altar candles* – Usually one to honour the Goddess and one for the God. They can also be represented by statues, pictures or other symbols.

- ❈ *Athame* – The Witches' knife or blade. Traditionally, a black-handled knife with a double-edged blade nine inches long, it is used when invoking and banishing the elements and other energies. Athames can also be made from horn, wood and other materials.

- ❈ *Chalice* – The Chalice is a symbol of the Goddess and can be made from wood, stone, glass or metal. It is used to contain the wine used in the Rite of Wine and Cakes, or in the Great Rite.

- ❈ *Boline* – The white-handled knife. This is the working knife of the Witch and is used whenever any cutting, say of herbs, or carving of symbols is required.

- ❈ *Wand* – A carefully collected and prepared piece of wood the length of its owner's forearm; it is also used for invoking and banishing.

- ❈ *Asperger* – A small bundle of twigs tied together to form a sort of mini-brush. An Asperger is used to sprinkle water, and sometimes oil, around an area.

magical methods

- *Besom* – The traditional Witches' broomstick. A symbol of fertility used in Handfasting, and to sweep away negative energies from the Circle or other areas.

- *Cauldron* – Used to contain fire for outdoor workings to protect the environment, and sometimes to contain water for scrying, it really should be made of metal, not plastic!

- *Cords* – Sometimes considered part of Altar equipment, they are used in Initiations and in cord and knot magic (see below).

- *Quarter lights* – Used to delineate the outer edges of the Circle for groups performing outdoor workings, although some use them inside to remind them where the Quarters lie.

- *Sword* – Used in group workings to cast the Circle, solitary Witches rarely use one of these, although many of us acquire one during the course of our working life. I personally feel self-conscious waving it around indoors or when on my own.

- *Scourge* – A feature primarily of Gardnerian Covens, it serves little purpose outside of formal groups.

There are other tools used by some individuals and groups such as the *staff* and *stang*, but these are less common these days. There are also practical pieces of equipment like matches, candle snuffers and so on, whose purposes are obvious, and there are items which make for safety, like secure candle holders and, if you intend to have a fire outdoors, enough water to hand to put it out. It goes, or should go, without saying that all magical tools are kept clean and in good condition if you wish them to work effectively.

the real witches' craft

PRACTICAL WORK 1

Consider all the magical tools which you have acquired during your time in the Craft, including any that you have in mind to get in the future. You can do this mentally, in a list, or actually get them out in front of you. Review the use(s) you have actually put them to; this can be interesting as we tend to use new things when we first get them but then to revert back to a far more limited selection of tried and trusted ones. Give some thought to how essential each really is to the working of your spells and, secondly, to how much support you feel you get from their presence when working.

As we each have our own preferences as to which of our working tools we feel attached to, there are no 'right' and 'wrong' answers to this. Lastly, imagine that you are away from home, with none of your tools, and need to work a spell. What substitutions could you use from the environment around you?

LINKS TO THE SUBJECT

If you are working for yourself, someone who you know well and who you can easily visualize, or who will actually be present, then you may need no physical links to the subject of your magic. But if it is someone distant, who you barely know, or may never even have met, then something which provides a tangible link can be really useful. Because it is our inner focus and energy which make the magic work, then the less of our attention and energy

involved in focusing on the subject, the more we have left for driving the magic. There are three basic types of link:

Images of the person – Where the subject of your spell is a person then probably the most useful link is a photograph. In the past a Witch might have created a fith-fath, or image of them using clay or wax. This would have been fashioned to look as much like the subject as possible. It may even have included hair and nail clippings, or a drop of their blood to enhance the link. Contrary to popular misconception, a fith-fath was not only used to curse or hex, but for any kind of magic including fertility and healing. Fith-faths are still used by some Witches today, and sometimes have a photograph of the subject's face pinned over the head. Whilst you could use hair and nail clippings if you wished, I would not recommend the use of blood as it is not safe these days. Even with a photograph or a fith-fath, some supplementary information will also help, for example, date of birth, star sign or favourite colour; anything in fact which helps to make this person real to you.

Object to represent a person – Occasionally, you may be asked to work magic for someone of whom you do not have even a reasonable physical description, in which case as much of the above-mentioned supplementary information as possible will help. With this information you can create an image or choose an object to represent your subject. For example, suppose you are asked to work for Anna, you have been given her date of birth and hence know her age and sun sign, you are told that she is keen on cats, loves the colour blue, and is fond of gardening. There are a number of ways you can incorporate this information into a spell for Anna. You could write her name in the middle of a blue sheet of paper, around that draw the sigil for her Sun sign and pictures of cats and flowers. Alternatively, you could engrave these signs onto a blue candle, or one the colour related to her Sun sign. You could choose a

gemstone, pebble or flower to represent her. Any of these options would be a good substitute for her actual image, but to increase the link you can also formally 'name' the object (see below).

Object to represent something – In much the same way you can also select an object or image to represent a thing or an idea rather than an individual. In some cases the choice is simple; a toy car to represent a real one, or a seashell to represent anything connected with the sea. If working for a particular species then it should be simple to find a photograph or picture, indeed if you have internet access then it's easy to find an image of almost anything. In other cases you may need to be a little more inventive, but the important thing is that the object should to you, and you alone, represent the thing you are working for. Again, this link can be increased by naming.

Naming an object

The process of naming is more or less the same, whether the link is a fith-fath, photograph or something you have created. Usually the object is prepared outside the Circle ahead of your Rites and the naming then takes place within the created Sacred Space as the first part of your spell. I prefer, wherever possible, to make the object the day before I work, as I find that an overnight meditation often helps to reinforce the following day's naming.

Once the Sacred Space has been created, the item is passed through each of the elements in turn with the words:

'I call upon the Element of Air (Fire, Water, Earth) to witness that I … (your own name) *do name this …* (name of your subject), *through the element of Air (Fire, Water, Earth). That it is become …* (name of subject) *within this Circle and within these Rites. As is my will so mote it be. Blessed Be.'*

Whilst you do this, visualize the essence of your subject entering and becoming one with your link. Obviously, you will have to make adjustments to the actual handling of some objects through the Elements. A solid can be dipped in the water whilst paper should only be sprinkled lightly; anything flammable or metallic should be passed over the candle flame not through it, and so on.

Once through the Elements you hold it up in both hands and present it to the Goddess and the God saying:

'Gracious Goddess, Mighty God, I … (your name) *do present this as …* (name of subject), *it having been named through the Elements of Air, Fire, Water and Earth and in your sight. May my magic worked upon it be carried truly to its rightful destination. Blessed Be.'*

To seal the naming, draw an invoking pentacle over the object. The invoking pentacle is, if likened to the numbers on a clock face, 12, 7, 3, 9, 5, 12; remember that you need the six points to complete the five lines of the pentacle.

the real witches' craft

Some Witches also like to consecrate the object with oil as a part of the naming, and if you choose to do this it is best done after it has been passed through the Elements but before you present it to the Goddess and the God. Anoint it with the oil at the points of an invoking pentagram and say:

'I do anoint thee with oil, precious to the Old Gods, that you now in truth be … (name of subject), *conduit for the passage of magic to* … (name the purpose of your spell). *Blessed Be.'*

Once the naming is complete you can then go on to perform the actual spell.

Where an object has been properly named within the Circle, it then becomes that person within the Circle and within any subsequent Circle. Any spell you work upon it will be transferred to the intended subject; this is sympathetic magic. Once it is out of the Circle you should keep it intact until you are sure that the spell has worked so that you may revisit it to reinforce the spell if necessary. But look after it carefully as it provides a strong connection to the subject, and its well-being is your responsibility. Accidental damage, perhaps by dropping, is not important as it is not done with magical intention, even if it is within the Circle. However, deliberate actions within a Circle will work even if performed by someone else. It's not just a question of trusting our fellow Witches; on one occasion someone I know thought a prepared fith-fath was unused and was only stopped from using it just in time. This kind of mistake can be more easily made with the less obvious forms like candles or stones. So best to be safe and sure!

magical methods

PRACTICAL WORK 2

Select three people you know well enough to be able to create magical links for. For each person, work out three different methods of creating magical links to them (you should end up with nine different links in all). Don't just use the ones from the text above; see if you can devise new ones. In each case, review how closely you feel that the link will relate to the person.

As with the tools exercise above, you will almost certainly find some are more comfortable to work with than others. Make sure your notes reflect which method(s) work best for you.

MAGICAL METHODS

These are not just the objects through which the magic happens, but also the ways of using them. Whilst I will talk about them as though they are separate here, and give some examples of their use, these are not exclusive; it is quite possible to adapt the methods described for one for use with another. It is equally possible to combine methods, or to create new ones. I have given brief examples of spells, but have not fully detailed them as you will already be familiar with the techniques necessary.

Candle magic

Candle spells are probably the most common form of magic for the solitary Witch, at least in part because they are easy to obtain and straightforward to use. They are also unlikely to cause comment from non-Witchy friends and family, being used by a lot of people for decorative purposes. They can be inscribed with sigils and/or anointed with oil to enhance their properties and can be used in conjunction with other things such as crystals. Candles can be selected by colour to enhance their purpose, although you can always use a white one for any kind of spell. It is thought by some that whole coloured candles will be more effective than those which merely have a layer of coloured wax outside of a white core. Most Witches keep a small stock of candles for magical use. Candles also have the advantage of being quick to put into use.

Examples of some types of candle spell include:

- *Healing* – Choose a candle either in a colour representative of the person, perhaps their favourite colour, or of lavender, the colour of healing. Anoint the candle with either a blend of oils specifically chosen for the person, or again with lavender oil. Note that anointing should start from the middle of the candle, moving out towards the ends. Don't use too much or the oil itself may catch light. Whilst anointing, visualize the person you are working for becoming stronger and their healing progressing quickly. Once the candle is anointed, hold it upright between both hands and breathe on it from bottom to top and back again, visualizing your breath, and therefore your intent, filling the candle. When this is done, set it in a safe holder and light it. Let it burn all the way down. If this is not possible, then relight it every day at around the same time, so that it is burnt away in three days.
- *Clear thought* – Select a yellow candle and inscribe it with the sigil of Air, for thought. About one third of the way down from the wick, tie a yellow thread with three knots, and cut the ends of the thread very close

to the knot, so that they do not trail. Light the candle and visualize your mind clearing and becoming focused. Place the candle in its holder onto a wide, fire-proof dish, a saucer works well, so that should the thread fall away from the candle, it will not set light to anything. Once the thread has been burnt, you may extinguish the candle and put it aside in case you want to re-work the spell at another time.

✸ *Reconciliation* – Take a pink candle and insert two pins into it, opposite each other, roughly halfway down. Light the candle and whilst it burns visualize both parties meeting and resolving their differences. When the candle burns down to the pins they will drop out, so put them to one side until the candle has completely burnt away. Once this has happened, either give one pin to each person, or place it somewhere they will be certain to pass over it regularly. This form of spell can provide the opportunity to make amends after a quarrel or disagreement, but it cannot guarantee reconciliation, especially if one or both parties is not really willing to make it up.

Once a candle has been prepared or used for a magical intent, it should not be used for any other purpose. If you prepare it for one spell but then use it for another you could get very mixed magic! You should also not use it for decorative lighting, unless you really want to reinforce the magic at that time. If you make your own candles, you can use left-over spell candles as long as you remember to do a banishing pentagram (using the clock face simile, this is 7, 12, 5, 9, 3, 7) over the molten wax.

No discussion of candle magic can go without mentioning safe use, as candles account for a significant and increasing number of house fires. Candles should always be placed in a steady holder on a safe surface, away from fabrics and strong air currents. Ideally, the stand should also be placed onto something fire-proof which will not be damaged by molten wax. If you are working with candles, place them in such a way that you will not have to reach over them for any reason. They should never be left unattended, and definitely never left burning whilst you sleep.

the real witches' craft

Fith-faths and Poppet magic

As mentioned above, fith-faths are usually made from wax or clay. The best are the ones you make yourself, as you visualize the purpose of the spell during the making. However, you can buy pre-made wax ones, some with an opening into which you can place further links to your subject. But do not be tempted by any which are made from man-made materials. Although the terms fith-fath and poppet are sometimes used interchangeably, poppets are usually made from cloth, preferably including some cloth used by the subject of the spell. They may have other links included in their stuffing, and/or symbols relating to the spell sewn into the fabric. Fith-faths and poppets are most useful if your spell needs to have a long duration, as in the examples below.

- ❀ *Fertility* – probably the most common use for a fith-fath is in fertility magic. Make one in the image of a heavily-pregnant woman for someone who would like to conceive. It is usual at this stage to tie a loose cord of red thread around her in order to secure the pregnancy, and this cord should be removed once the pregnancy has run its proper course in order to facilitate birth. A fith-fath can be inscribed with the initials of the woman, or of the couple, and named.
- ❀ *Prosperity* – dress your poppet in green and use gold and silver threads to embroider symbols of prosperity and of security. You could also sew on small coins, and metallic buttons to symbolize money.

Amulets and Talismans

Generally, amulets are three-dimensional objects such as jewellery or small items; they can also be gemstones, pebbles or small images made from clay or the like. Talismans are usually made from paper, parchment or fabric. As with many magical terms there is quite a lot of cross-over between them. Both are intended to carry long term, on-going spells, such as those for protection, or

magical methods

to make a permanent change. When they are for personal use, an amulet is often intended to be worn, whereas a talisman is more likely to be carried, possibly in the wallet. Obviously, in this case the choice will be made depending on whether a person feels more comfortable wearing jewellery or carrying a paper on their person. Where they are used to protect an object such as a house or car, then the choice will depend upon the practicalities. My home is protected by a parchment talisman over the door; this is because a hanging object near the entrance would almost certainly prove too tempting for the cats! The car, on the other hand, has an amulet, as it tends to get damp inside and anything organic would not fare well.

- ❀ *Increasing self-confidence* – Take a piece of rose quartz, either loose or in a piece of jewellery, and empower it in the Circle by passing it through the Elements. This is done in a similar way to that of naming but instead of giving the object a name, you give it the energy for its purpose.

- ❀ *Household security* – You will need to create a talisman for each of the entrances to your home. Make a circle of stiff golden-coloured paper a couple of inches across. In the centre, draw a picture of your home and around this draw images of all the people and animals living there with you. Your images do not have to be works of art, but should be recognizable to you. Take this into the Circle and empower it in the same way as above. Once you have done this, draw a circle in red ink around all the images, close to the outer edge of the paper. Turn the paper over and draw a pentagram on the reverse side, invoking the protection of the Goddess and the God as you do so. Once your Ritual is complete place the talismans over the entrances to your home. It used to be recommended that you bury them under the outside of the doorway, but these days there are few homes where this would be practical.

the real witches' craft

Other Paper and Parchment spells

Paper and/or parchment can also be put to good use in spells for ridding yourself of the unwanted, like old habits, long-term regrets, and much else. Details of the issue are written out and the paper can be burnt, and the ashes buried or allowed to dispel on the wind, or they can be shredded and consigned to the flowing water of a river or the sea.

❀ *To conclude an outworn relationship* – Sometimes we get to the end of a relationship with someone, yet seem to be unable to stop reliving or revisiting it. It can happen because of divorce, other break-ups and even bereavement. It can even be the case after a non-personal relationship; work, business, or anything else which leaves a deep impression. And these thoughts can prevent us moving forwards cleanly into the rest of our lives. Write down, on thin paper, all your thoughts and feelings relating to this issue in as much detail as you can. It can be best to do this over a few days, so as to include everything. Take the paper to a place by running water and read it through thoroughly. Then tear it into tiny pieces, and let these go into the water. As you do so, visualize the water flowing to the sea and the waters there washing away all your cares and concerns. Once you have done this, take some of the water and literally wash your hands of the issue.

Sachets

Another form of long-term spell is the use of sachets. These are usually small bags made of a fabric in a colour appropriate to the purpose and filled with a blend of herbs specific to your intent. Sachets can be hung in rooms or in vehicles; they can be placed in the bed, carried or even worn. They are a good way of giving a spell to another, so that they can choose when to use it.

@ *Healing sleep* – Take a circle of lavender-coloured fabric about six inches across. Into the centre place some dried lavender, chamomile and a few sea salt crystals. Gather the edges up and secure with a lavender-coloured ribbon. Do not make the bundle too tight, as it needs to be soft enough to go under a pillow. Empower it within the Circle by passing it through the Elements. If you are going to be giving it to another, wrap it carefully in tissue paper before you complete the Ritual.

Cord and Knot magic

Cords and knots have long been used as a way of giving delayed-action and step-by-step spells. Probably the best-known is the wind spell traditionally given to sailors. In this, a cord with three knots is prepared and empowered. The sailor then undoes one, two, or all three knots, depending on the strength of the wind required. But this is not the full extent of cord magic; it can be used to create spells which take place in stages for all aspects of life. We talk about cord magic, but in reality anything which can be knotted can be used; thread, rope, or even hair. If the spell requires the knots to be undone, then obviously the medium should be thick enough to allow un-knotting. Ideally, you should use natural, not synthetic materials for cord and knot magic, and the only knots should be those for magical purposes; the ends of a cord need to be sewn over rather than knotted.

@ *Memory spell* – When you have a series of things to remember, make a list and take this and a fine yellow cord into the Circle. For each item on the list visualize it, and say it aloud three times, whilst placing a knot in your cord. When all the knots have been made, consecrate the cord through the Elements, and carry it until you have no further need of it.

@ *Healing swellings on limbs* – To reduce the pain and swelling caused by a strain or sprain, tie black and red cord loosely around the affected part

the real witches' craft

overnight. Make sure that it cannot constrict the flow of blood. In the morning, take the cord and bury it to the north side of your home. Over the site of the buried cord, draw a banishing pentagram.

Correspondences and Sigils

Two other kinds of magical methods which sometimes come up in questions are correspondences and sigils.

- ❀ *Correspondences* are simply links from one thing to another, for example the colour of a candle is often chosen to relate to its subject, perhaps lavender for healing, or green for fertility, and so on. Whilst correspondences can be useful in much the same way as links to the person, their use is not essential. If you find them helpful, all is well and good, but you do not have to spend hours memorizing tables of them in order to be able to work spells.
- ❀ *Sigils* are written symbols which can be created by a Witch to represent a particular thing, much in the same way that a marketing company may design a logo to represent the company or the product. A sigil may be designed using a person's initials and carved into a candle used on their behalf, or it could be created to represent the spell itself.

As with the other methods it is not the use of these things which makes your magic work, it is the way in which you use them.

Other Methods

There are too many other ways of performing spells to go into detail about all of them here, but many of these are covered in my other books. In reality, you can empower almost anything to perform a spell; any of the above, and also less obvious things: spells to be given to another can be put into plants, or handmade gifts. Healing for close family and friends can often be worked by cooking something containing healing herbs and then empowering it. Soaps, bath salts, perfumes and the like can also be used as the medium for transferring a spell. You could empower a CD or cassette, jewellery, flowers, or even chocolates. Because your spell could be carried in almost anything, it's important that you use your magic wisely and safely, otherwise you could find that your every gift is considered with suspicion. After all, it is sometimes said that you should be wary of accepting a gift from a Witch, unless you trust them very well, as you may not know what has been added to it!

PRACTICAL WORK 3

Think of a relatively straightforward spell that you would be likely to perform, or if you have one in mind to work anyway, use this as your starting point. Consider how you could work this spell with each of the above methods. If you can, see if you can come up with other ways of performing it. Think about ways you might give it to someone else, both in person and by post, and also a 'time-delayed' version, so that they could start it up at a time when they want to.

If you have kept a Book of Shadows you may also find it useful to go back over your previous workings and consider which other ways you could have worked some of these.

Magical methods are only limited by your imagination and your ability to use them to focus your energy. There are no 'correct' tools, links or objects for working magic, despite what you may have heard. Imagine you were able to travel freely in time and space: is it likely that the Witches, Shamans and other magical workers of old, from Europe, Asia, Australasia, the Americas, and so on, would have used the same tools, methods and techniques? Well, obviously it isn't. There would have been physical, cultural and even legal differences. Today's Witches, likewise, have differences, even within the same region, let alone from different countries. They even have differences between one stage of their Craft and another; Today, I may use many different herbs and plants from my garden, but there has been a time when nearly all my spells were conducted using candles because I had no garden. And, as I mentioned earlier,

magical methods

we each develop preferences for different forms of working. But whilst it is good to use those things which are tried and tested for you, it is also good to remind yourself that there are other ways. If you don't you could find that your magic becomes stale or, even worse, that you are unable to think of new ways when the ones you have become accustomed to are, for some reason, unavailable to you.

But for every Witch, there are times when you cannot work with tangible objects. You may be away on holiday, visiting friends, or just out for the day. Under these circumstances you may not be able to light a candle, let alone make and name a fith-fath. This is where you need to be able to rely on being able to work on an entirely different plane.

Chapter Nine

WORKING
ON THE ASTRAL

In one respect, all of our Ritual and magical work means working on the astral plane. The Sacred Space we create in the here and now is also created on the astral, and the energies we use in our spells come from and work through it. The astral plane is not another place, or location, in the same way that one country is different from another, but rather another part of existence.

When we cast the Circle we talk about 'a place between the worlds and a time out of time', and this reflects the fact that the Circle is in both worlds, that of the physical and that of the spirit. The astral is a different aspect of where we are now, and it is linked to both past and future. It is everywhere and nowhere, and it is everywhen. There are no special words, signs, potions or incenses which will automatically transfer us from this plane to the other; it is more a question of transferring our inner energy or self. Whilst this may seem daunting, remember that the various states of meditation take us to the astral, as can our power raising, Circle casting and other magical techniques. Having said that, most people use the term Astral Workings to denote those which take place fully in the spiritual, rather than in both worlds.

The psychic plane, or level, is not entirely the same as the astral. Psychic work includes all kinds of divination, where the energies you utilize are linked to the astral but just as closely connected with accessing the inner self. As with many forms of magical terminology the two often cross over and are sometimes used interchangeably. The difficulty is that there are actually many planes of being, rather like the layers of an onion. They meet and touch in many ways, and sometimes the boundaries are not distinct, but blur and merge, just as the boundaries between waking, sleeping and dreaming can.

Witches, and many other magical practitioners, often work on the astral. There we can create permanent working sites, for personal or group use. We can travel on the astral from one place to another, and utilize it to seek information, as well as knowledge of different times. There are also some kinds of magic, such as the creation of thought-forms, which can only take place on the astral. It is also said that a portion of the working personae of every Witch will remain on the astral even after death, not as a personality which could be contacted through séances and the like, but as an energy-form.

Before talking about actually working on these levels, it is as well to be aware of some cautions: there are entities and energy-forms on the astral which have their own existence. Sometimes these are the remnants of unfinished workings, or they may have been created by magical workers and not properly banished. Most are harmless, but some will still seek to complete the work they were created for, and this may not always be beneficial to you. Not everyone who works on the astral abides by the Wiccan Rede; there are those who work in this way who have entirely different beliefs and aims. For these reasons it is as well to be properly protected before commencing any form of astral work, and to ensure that you are careful about your actions there. It's not just a question of having your magic interfered with, it is possible to bring unwelcome energies back with you into the physical, and as someone once commented: 'Anything you allow to follow you home from the astral is unlikely to be housebroken!'

the real witches' craft

PRACTICAL WORK 1
— THE CIRCLE WITHIN

As you are already aware, the Circle is your greatest protection and earlier I talked about creating a sacred space which you can then absorb within yourself. But it is a good idea to practise this on a regular basis and especially before working on the astral.

Invoke each of the Elements in your usual way but using visualization, and once you have them all in balance and firmly in mind, go on to invite the Goddess and the God, and cast the Circle. When all is in place, draw the Circle in towards you, until it forms a sort of second skin just over, or just under, your own. At this point you need to fix it in place by attaching it to your skin. Once it is securely in place, and as long as you keep it there, then you are protected on all the astral and psychic planes.

Whilst this sounds relatively simple, it does take a little practice to actually keep the Circle in place. It's a good idea to practise this a few times whilst carrying out your normal activities. Create the Circle, secure it, and then carry on as usual for an hour or so, every so often take a moment to check that it is still intact. You should be able to do this by closing your eyes and 'looking' to see if the electric blue light is still there as strongly as it was when you cast the Circle. On your first attempts you may detect thin patches or even holes. If this is so, reinforce it and then carry on to the end of your allotted period. With practice you will be able to maintain the Circle for days at a time, although it is best to only use the technique when you actually need

it as it does constitute a drain on your energy. Always take the Circle down completely when you have finished with it, however thin and patchy you may feel it has become.

Of course, whilst the Circle will protect you on the astral, it will only do so as long as your actions there do not invite the wrong sort of attention. It is important to remain focused on the intention of your journey or visit, and not to become distracted by anything else you may encounter. Energies or entities on the astral often appear attractive, or deliberately invite the curious. Their existence and sometimes their purpose can draw energy from the attention paid to them. They can interfere with the purpose of your journey and may, rarely, cause harm to your psyche. Should you become overly involved with them it is possible for some of their energy to return with you to the here and now. Whilst this can sound alarming, remember that it rarely happens, and is unlikely to do so as long as you protect yourself and remain focused whilst you work. If you think back to your earlier days in the Craft you may remember reading or being told that you should not work magic when weakened by illness, distracted or unable to remain in balance, as all of these things can leave you less able to handle aspects of working on the astral. It cannot be stressed enough that the astral is not a good place to fool around in.

THE ASTRAL TEMPLE

For these and other reasons, those who work regularly on the astral will create their own Sacred Space, or Astral Temple there. Not only does this provide a secured working space, but some individuals or groups may choose to use it as a meeting place when physical meetings are difficult or even impossible. Most of us do not have the space in our homes or gardens to create a working space which can be left as that alone. Generally, we are lucky if we can retain a small part of a shelf or windowsill where we can leave a couple of candles and perhaps a spell in progress, without risking it being looked at by non-Witchy friends and family, or even worse, being fiddled with by the curious. And even if everyone you know understands to leave such things alone, there's still the playful cat, or unexpected visitor to contend with. So a Sacred Space on the astral for working, meditating, or even just for relaxation, is the ultimate secure location.

One of the other advantages of an Astral Temple is that there are few limits as to how you design it. Unlike your home, you can have as much space as you wish; you're not constrained by the size or shape of your rooms. You can choose to have an indoor or outdoor working space, or even one which is partly both. It could resemble a place you know in the physical realm, or could be created entirely from your imagination. The only real constraint occurs if you intend to share it with others, as they too will need to be able to visualize it as clearly as you. To give you some ideas, the following are just two scenarios from which you could draw some inspiration:

The first: Imagine yourself standing in the centre of a wide, circular glade in the forest. The ground is covered by lush green grass, and around the edge are trees waving gently in the breeze. To the north of this circle is a large stone with a flat surface, its edges carved with engravings of the Goddess and the God. This stone is your Altar and in the centre there is a small dish containing a fire which never goes out. You can place any tools and equipment you need to use on this Altar. The outer boundary of the Circle is marked by a faintly glowing light, which protects it at all times and will let none through save those who you choose to allow entry.

The second: Imagine yourself standing before a large oak door. In your hand you have a small plain brass key. Use the key to open the door, and then close it carefully behind you. In front of you is a large square room, its floor a mosaic of tiles leading in spirals both into and out of the centre. The walls are hung with tapestries, and at each of the quarters these show the Goddess and the God through

working on the astral

the seasons of the year. At the far end of the room is an Altar flanked by two flaming torches. On it stand statues of the Goddess and the God, a Chalice of wine, a censer with smoking incense, a bowl of water and a small dish of salt. On the walls of the room are many, many shelves holding all the books, herbs and other magical supplies which you use in your workings.

Neither of the above are definitive ideas, nor are they as complete as you might like to make them. But in both cases you will notice that there are special ways in which they are protected from outsiders or from other energies; in the first it is the Circle as you would usually cast it, in the second it is the key, which only you have. When preparing your Astral Temple, it is important to remember to include this way of 'locking' the space. Another consideration is your method of entry; you may choose to walk a particular route or to simply arrive at the entrance. Personally, I prefer to approach my Astral Temple from a distance. This has several advantages; first, it allows time to adjust to working on this plane. But secondly, and just as important, it allows the opportunity to see whether any changes have occurred since your last visit. If you share this space with others, you can arrange for certain signs and symbols to be in place to identify whether the space is in use, or has been used. Approaching slowly also allows you to see whether other energies might be present in the vicinity.

It is also a good idea to always make your entry point to the astral plane the same, or at least limit it to one or two points, whatever you intend to do when you get there. This gives you a permanent reference point, or a couple of points, to work with. Choosing too many different entrances can be disorienting, especially as you should always leave by the same point at which you entered, every time. Again you can choose your entry and leaving paths. It could be a remembered or imaginary street which you walk down until you come to the point at which you switch from the physical to the astral, or a footpath through the countryside. You could even select to make the entrance from your own home, perhaps through a doorway which in the physical may lead to a cupboard, but in your meditation will lead onto the astral, although some people feel that this is a little too close for comfort! Whichever kind of entrance you choose to enter the astral, this portal, or doorway, should always be sealed after you. Not only on the way out; to prevent anything following you, but also on your way in, as you don't want something unexpected to slip past you and await your return.

Having thought in abstract about the type of Astral Temple you would like to create, the next step is to give some thought to the details. Start by deciding how large you would prefer your Temple to be, bearing in mind whether you will be inviting others to join you in working there.

This may be the point to mention that you should never invite anyone to work with you on the astral if you haven't already worked with them, in person, in the physical realm several times. And never, ever, invite anyone into your Astral Temple if your only acquaintance is through the internet and perhaps one or two casual meetings. Inviting someone into your Astral Temple is pretty nearly the same as inviting them to have free access to the inside of your mind unless you have extremely powerful defences in place.

But to return to creating your Temple, once you have chosen its structure, give some thought as to what you would like to put inside in terms of permanent fixtures (temporary ones can be introduced as and when you want to use them). It is usual to have an Altar, and to leave at least one light burning in the Temple at all times, but you may like to include other things; perhaps shelves, seats or cushions, torches, a fire or brazier, and so on. Of course, you can continue to furnish your Temple as you use it, but it's helpful to have a rough idea of how much you may want to keep there, so that you can ensure it is created large enough.

Once you have the 'structure' of your Temple in mind, then you can go on to decide your approach and your entrance way. This may seem like planning backwards but it's usually more effective to choose the approaches to suit the

working on the astral

Temple, rather than the other way around. It's a good idea to plan the approach in as much, if not more, detail than the Temple itself, as this is a part of the process of moving from the physical to the astral. Don't restrict yourself to just the pathway itself but extend your view to what is around you. Define the scene as well as you can, giving some thought as to how it might change through different times of the day, and seasons of the year. It is a good idea to delineate the actual entry to your Temple with some form of locking device: this can be a key, an opening of the Circle, a spiral which you trace, or any other device which you use as a form of coded entrance. In addition to approaching your Temple through meditation, you can also set into place a simpler form of entry, such as counting backwards in twos, or a specific chant or mantra, but these would be approaches you only use when your Temple is established and you are familiar with its use.

PRACTICAL WORK 2
— CREATING YOUR ASTRAL TEMPLE

Once you have considered the layout, decoration, approach and entry to your Temple you can set about establishing it. The best time is during the later part of the waxing Moon, just before the full Moon. Select a time when you will be undisturbed, turning off the phone if you feel this will help. Take your notes on your Temple and read them through thoroughly, making any last minute changes you feel are necessary, although try to keep these to the minimum. As this is a somewhat detailed and lengthy visualization it is important that you undertake it when you are both fit and rested. Using the above technique, create the Circle Within. Then, using the relaxation and pathworking techniques create your path to the location of your Astral Temple. Once there, expand your inner Circle before starting to create the Temple within its boundary.

First, visualize the structure of your temple and once you feel that it is established, repeat the creation of the Sacred Space within your Astral Temple. Call the Elements, invite the Goddess and the God and cast the Circle. Take your time with this and do it thoroughly. You may wish to visualize yourself actually making the invoking pentagrams and saying the words. You may like to expand upon this by lighting candles at the quarters or by placing elemental symbols or objects at them. For example, you could visualize placing a besom or broomstick in the East, lighting a torch or fire in the South, filling a cauldron with water in the West and placing a monolith, or even erecting a stone Altar, in the North. Equally, you can create and/or place objects to represent the

working on the astral

Goddess and the God, or you could ask them to bring representations with them; perhaps a Willow tree for the Goddess and an Oak for the God. Although you would probably not do it on the physical, you might also like to mark out your Circle with salt, chalk or some other boundary, before expanding it above and below. You are, in effect, creating a Circle within a Circle, the former being that of the Temple, the latter being your own personal one, which you will later take away within you again.

With the structure and Circle in place, focus on your locking device(s). Just as when you need to enter or leave a cast Circle you open and close it behind you each time, then your Astral Temple should be unlocked and then locked behind you whenever you enter or leave. However, unlike a Circle cast on the physical, you will not be dismissing the Elements, or removing the Circle before you leave. The Goddess and the God, however, should always be thanked at the end of each use. With all secured you can then focus on the more decorative aspects, tools and other equipment. On this occasion include on your Altar salt, water and some anointing oil, in addition to those things you would normally place there.

Once all is ready, it is time to consecrate your Temple. Take the anointing oil and ask the blessing of the Goddess and the God, that the oil might bring their blessings on everything it touches. Use this to anoint your hands, feet and forehead, and then the Altar. Add some salt to the water, and ask the Goddess and the God to likewise bless it, that it might cleanse and consecrate everything it touches. Take this and sprinkle it around the boundary of your Sacred Space and on everything within the Temple. As you do so, visualize each object glowing with an inner light and becoming Sacred to this Temple and to your use. Once you have finished, place both oil and salted water in a safe place within your Temple. As and when you bring new objects here then you can use them again to consecrate and bless.

If you have any magical work or spells which you wish to perform in your Temple at this time, you can go on to do so, or you can simply remain here in meditation for a while if you wish to. Once you are ready to leave, remember to thank the Goddess and the God and to tidy the area as you would a physical space. Then re-absorb your inner Circle. On future visits you will not normally need to expand and reabsorb this as the Circle within the Temple will remain there. Unlock the entrance and, locking it again behind you, proceed down your route until you return to the here and now. Remember to write this up in your journal.

Assuming all went according to plan, your Astral Temple is now ready and available for use. If, however, you have any doubts about how successful you were, then leave it at least twenty-four hours before trying again. Your subsequent attempts need to start from the beginning, unless you are totally confident that you have completed up to and including the consecration of all the objects within the Temple. This is to avoid leaving any weaknesses in the security of your working space on the Astral. You can use an Astral Temple at any time, although it may take you some practice to become as familiar as you have been with your more usual way of working. In the early days of using your Temple it's a good idea to try to visit at least once a week, in order to familiarize yourself with it, even if you only visit to spend a few moments in contemplation. Of course, you can start using it to work spells and magic as soon as you feel comfortable doing so. Some Witches use their Temple in preference to physical working, especially if they find it difficult to work undisturbed at home. It can also be a good way of achieving the benefits of outdoor working when this is not practical.

Of course, thus far I have really only talked about using an Astral Temple as a solitary Witch, but as mentioned earlier, you can also use one as a meeting and working place with others. There are two basic ways of doing so. You

working on the astral

can open your personal Temple to those you trust, or you can create one for joint or group use. The latter is the preferable option as it keeps your own separate for you, whilst giving you the alternative of a group one. Temples for group working can be created jointly, although this usually takes quite a lot of discussion, or by one person who then takes the other(s) there using guided meditation. It's worth remembering, though, that even if you only take someone to an Astral Temple once, then they will always be able to return, even if you subsequently change your mind about them. Astral Temples for group working often tend to be larger and somewhat more formalized, as obviously the more detail you have, the harder it is to communicate it to others. Should you decide to make an Astral Temple available to someone else, then you need to impress upon them that the invitation is only open to them; they're not supposed to pass it on to others unless you permit it. There is, after all, no reason why they can't create their own if they want to share. If your Temple is for joint use, then each user must be aware of the need to approach somewhat more sensitively in case it is already occupied by another. Some groups will arrange signals on the approach or at the entrance to alert others when they use it, and experienced users will be able to detect and identify the shift in energies caused by other users anyway.

This shift in energies is also a way of identifying whether your Temple has been approached by anyone or anything else on the astral. Usually it will manifest itself by a displacement of things on the approach; this is why you need to be familiar with the route and entrance. This can be the addition or removal of things, or simply their movement. Sometimes it can take the form of changes in the appearance or feeling of things along the way. Should you notice such changes as you approach, then pass them by, then when you are securely in your Temple, expand your inner Circle until you have reinforced the boundaries by recreating the Sacred Space there. You may feel that I'm implying that work on the astral is particularly hazardous, but really this is not the case. Just as when working in the physical realm you are protected by normal security measures, such as closing your front door, not inviting strangers home, and working within your Sacred Space, you can easily protect yourself on the astral. It's just that it can be easier to forget the basic preparations when working in a new environment.

It is worth visiting your Temple at different phases of the Moon and at different times of the day, and noting the differences in the surroundings and the energies present. Once you have become accustomed to these you will be able to alter them to suit your workings, and visit the astral at times which are not the same as those on the physical. Probably the easiest way of achieving this is to use your approach as a period where you move through time as well as travel your route. Imagine one of those pieces of film where time-lapse photography has been used to speed up the passage of time. The clouds move rapidly across the sky, the day changes from day to night and back to day again in a few minutes. If you visualize this on the astral you can actually change the time of day there. With practice you can also change the time of the year, or even the year itself, although the further from 'now' you attempt to travel the less accurate your impressions will be.

PRACTICAL WORK 3
— CHANGING TIMES

Prepare yourself in the usual way by forming the Circle within and start on your route to your Temple. As you go pause for a moment and move time forward from the 'now'; if you started in the day, go forward to the night or vice versa. Once you feel you have achieved the time change, complete your route to the Temple and compare your impressions to see if they match those you have felt when actually visiting at this time of day in the physical world. On your return journey from the Temple, remember to reverse the process to bring you back to the time of day in the physical.

It's best to reverse any changes in time as otherwise you may upset your internal body rhythms. As with some of the other skills and techniques of the Craft, some people find it comes easily, whereas others may have to practise before they find that what they are envisaging becomes actual. Part of the difficulty is that our minds are capable of operating on several levels at once, and when trying out something new a part of the brain acts as an observer. In order for magic to take place or for work on the astral, all of the mind needs to be focused on the task at hand. So if you find yourself wondering when you'll feel or notice 'something different', be aware that this indicates you are not fully focused. It's a bit like 'trying' to fall asleep: the more you think about falling asleep the more wakeful you'll feel, but if you focus your thoughts on not 'observing' the falling-asleep process, then you sleep. Likewise, if you can focus only on the work you are doing on the astral, then it will happen.

Of course, creating and using a Temple is just one aspect of working on the astral. Once you are comfortable visiting and using your Temple then you can go on to other ways of working there. One of the more frequently mentioned is Astral Travel, which enables you to visit other places. These can be places on that plane, or other locations on the physical. Certainly, when practising it is a good idea to start by visiting familiar places. Astral Travel can be used to visit fellow Witches, to check on the results of spells, and even, when combined with movement through time, to check on the potential results of magic. It should not be used to 'spy' or to over-look others, and it's worth noting that even the least sensitive person can usually tell when they are being overlooked, even if they can't actually explain their feelings.

ASTRAL TRAVEL

Astral Travel, or Astral Projection, is best explained by saying that you are separating your mental, or astral, and physical selves and using your mind only to go from one place to another. As with any other work on the astral this is perfectly safe as long as you remember to protect yourself before you start. Contrary to the things you may read in some fiction, your body is not at risk of possession from 'dark forces' whilst you travel, nor is your body at risk from external forces on the physical, as you will find that you will 'snap back' to the present should there be any interruption, such as someone entering the room or the phone ringing, although you may feel slightly disorientated for a moment or two if this happens unexpectedly. Equally, you are not going to get lost on the astral. Many people report seeing their mental and physical selves being joined by a line or cord of light, but some do not see this visually, they are simply aware of this strong attachment. Many people consider that it is far easier to do this if you make a conscious effort to try not to look at your astral self, as this act of observation can get in the way of focusing on what you are trying to do. Some people describe the moment of 'separation' as being a sort of sideways shift, or even jolt, although for others it can be a very smooth transition. A good many people find that, as soon as

working on the astral

they realize they have actually managed this, they seem to automatically return to their physical self. Certainly this seems to be almost universal on the first few attempts, but do persevere.

In your early practice, try moving from one room to another in your own home. Whilst in time you can practise doing this by moving through the astral, you may find it easier to actually visualize the journey from one place to another as you would make it in reality. So, if you are working in your room you would send your mental self across the room, down the corridor or stairs and into another room.

PRACTICAL WORK 4

Prepare yourself as you would for visiting your Astral Temple. Then visualize yourself rising up out of your physical body so that you are floating over it. Look down and observe the way your physical form is lying, or sitting, notice the things around you and the feeling of being as light as air. Now take yourself from this location to another room in your house, recalling the steps and route as though you were doing this on the physical. If you can, choose a room where someone else has been since your last visit there – this is helpful as you will be able to look around and see whether they have moved anything. Once you have visited, return by the same route and simply allow yourself to drift downwards back into your physical self. When you are ready, open your eyes and either rub your arms and legs, or have something to eat or drink to ground yourself properly. Once you have done so, make a point of physically visiting the room that you explored to check whether it is the same as you experienced on your travel.

The above exercise is more easily conducted if you have a trusted Witch-friend to work with, as you can ask them to make a deliberate adjustment to the specified location, or you can share the exercise by taking it in turns to visit one another. If you have previously created a protective Circle around your room or house you will need to open a temporary doorway in this to allow access, and to close it again later. If you are on the receiving end of a planned visit then try to relax with your eyes closed and see if you can detect

their presence. It can be useful if you both note down your experiences and exchange notes, as in discussion it can be possible for one person's recollection to colour that of the other.

From time to time you may notice that when working and travelling on the astral your feet do not actually touch the ground, or that you glide down, or up, stairs rather than stepping. You will also find that you can move through walls, floors or ceilings and so forth. None of these are barriers on the astral. And, as you become more comfortable with the experience, you can take short cuts through such physical obstacles. Indeed, after a bit of practice you will find that you can simply decide upon your destination in order to find yourself there.

You may notice shadowy forms around you on your travels. Generally speaking these are best left alone. When you have been working in this way for some while, you may find that you can recognize and identify some of these, at which point you can decide whether or not you wish to interact with them in any way. As mentioned before, there are many different entities which you may encounter and this is probably the time to look at some of the more commonly encountered ones.

✹ *Residual energies* – You are most likely to encounter general energies rather than actual beings or entities on the astral. These may be left over from magical acts which have not been fully completed or cleared away. This is one of the reasons for clearing away magically, like banishing those things you invoke and so on, or they can be caused by strong emotional responses. They have no consciousness or self-awareness and generally speaking will dissipate in time. Sometimes they can attach themselves to a person working on the astral and may even be felt on your return to the physical. Like other unwanted energies it is usually their effects, rather than any manifestation, which you notice and they can be banished fairly simply as you will see in the last chapter of this book.

❀ *Other magical workers* – If you spend much time on the astral you may, from time to time, notice the presence of others who are also working there, although it is more usual to become aware that they have been in the vicinity rather than to actually encounter them. Even if you think you recognize someone, it is better not to interact with them unless this was previously agreed between you, as it can deflect you from your intent, and they may not be who or what they appear.

❀ *Spirit forms* – Some magical workers create spirit forms as a part of their magic. These are entities which have no personal volition but are charged with a purpose which they must complete before they can dissipate. Rarely, these are even created to be negative in intent. Some spirit forms may also have been enabled to draw energy from other magical workers, which is one of the reasons why they are best avoided. Sometimes these forms may be created as protectors for individuals or even for places and things, in which case they may react quite strongly should you attempt to interfere with whatever or whoever they are guarding. If you find yourself unable to access a particular place, or to go in a particular direction on the astral, there is a good chance that one of these guardians is in place. In this case it is best to return home and try another day, or, if you really need, to attempt another route. Sometimes, spirit forms are perceived as having a physical presence; at other times it is their effects which alert you to their existence.

In addition, you may sometimes come across the term 'spirit guide'. Some consider that there are beings on the astral who are either pre-determined, or can be persuaded to act as guides in the spiritual realm. Generally speaking, these are used by Spiritualists and Mediums to provide links between the worlds of the living and the dead. As it is not a part of the Craft to summon, or call upon, the spirits of those who have died, Witches do not, on the whole, use spirit guides. You may, however, occasionally notice them on the astral. Spirit guides are not the same as Totem animals, which may accompany you on the astral and will serve the purpose of companion and protector.

On the subject of spirits and the spirit world, it is worth mentioning that it is never a good idea to use a ouija board or planchette. This is usually a board or cloth with letters and numbers on it. A glass or a pointer is used to allow entities from the spirit world to communicate with those using the board. As it means opening a door into the spirit world and encouraging whatever may be on the other side to come through, it can be extremely hazardous. Generally speaking, the sort of entities which actively seek admittance to our world are highly unlikely to be benign.

Sometimes, although infrequently, the astral or psychic planes leak into our subconscious through our dreams. This is why some dreams can be predictive or can give us otherwise hidden knowledge. Having said that, the vast majority of dreams are far more likely to be related to our daily existence. It is often maintained that dreams are the mind's way of sorting through our daily experiences and if you bear this in mind you can often find a mundane explanation for even the most seemingly auspicious of dreams. For example, my partner's Totem animal is the magpie, and the other night I dreamt of two magpies, surely a sign of good fortune? Well, it could be, but I somewhat suspect it's more likely to be a memory connected with a TV commercial for dishwasher tablets which likewise featured two magpies! So, whilst it is worth seeking the relevance of dreams, it is equally worth remembering that very few will have a deeper significance than a reflection of the mundane.

Another form of astral travel is shape-shifting, the ability to become a bird or animal. This is not the shape-shifting of werewolf movies and special effects, where a person literally transforms into an animal, usually losing their human personality and becoming a 'monster' in the process. Rather, it is a question of putting a part of your mind into that of the animal in question, alongside their own. Older Witches often refer to it as 'riding' and another fairly accurate term has been coined by author Terry Pratchett's fictional witch, Granny Weatherwax, who refers to it as 'borrowing'. This is usually done to experience the world through the eyes of the animal in question, and to gain insights from their perspective. It can also be interesting to see things through

the eyes of your Totem animal. It is undoubtedly easier and more effective to do this with a pet, or even better, your Familiar; certainly it is a good idea to start with an animal with which you have a strong bond. Later, when you're more familiar with the technique, you may choose to work with other animals, birds, and so on.

This is probably the time to mention the differences between a pet and a Familiar: First, however much you love them and however significant a role they play in your life, not every pet is, or can become a Familiar. Nor for that matter need every Familiar be a pet. A pet is an animal with which you share your life, caring for its physical and emotional needs in exchange for its uncritical love and devotion, which strikes me as an arrangement that we benefit greatly from. A Familiar is an animal with whom you share your spiritual and magical life. It could be an animal within the household, or just as likely be one which exists only on the astral. In some cases much loved pets do become Familiars, but many do not, and it is not fair to try to force any animal to become a Familiar if it is not in their temperament. It is rare for very young animals to be Familiars; in fact they may often not become so until they are quite mature.

Probably the easiest way to determine whether your pet is also going to be your Familiar is whether you notice that they accompany you on the astral. Other signs include an obvious and seemingly intelligent interest in your magical work on the physical, and this doesn't just mean turning up when the feasting starts! A true Familiar will turn up voluntarily, every time you commence any form of working, but will not interrupt, get in the way, or make off with your wand. They will also seek you out when you are meditating, and may well be by your side when you are reading or studying the Craft too.

When working with any kind of animal you need to remember that they have their own lives and it's important not to interfere with the natural rhythms of these. If you ride in the mind of another, their safety will depend on them

working on the astral

being able to utilize all of their natural instincts and abilities. Whilst you can suggest direction and destination you need to be careful not to take them into dangerous places, or to expose them to predators or other dangers. For example, you should not try to take a cat across a busy road, or through the garden of a large dog. Whilst you might be in their mind because you are working on the astral, their body will still be operating in the physical. For these reasons you should start by being a passive passenger, until you become familiar with the world from their perspective.

One of the best ways of beginning to work with shape shifting is to take your pet onto your lap, or beside you on the bed, and pet them until both you and they are very relaxed. Whilst focusing on your pet, allow your spiritual form to drift and to sense their thoughts, which are likely to be of the interaction between you. If your pet moves away or seems to become uncomfortable then stop immediately and try another time. After a few attempts you should find that you start to feel your surroundings from their perspective. It's worth remembering that cats and dogs have far more acute hearing and sense of smell than humans. Dogs in particular perceive smell in a completely different way, similar to highly coloured auras, whilst their perception of physical colour is almost non-existent.

Once you have done this a few times you will find that it becomes easier to become tuned in to your pet and you can then move into their mind at other times. Try feeding time, and other activities around the home as your next step. And then, when you are both comfortable, try excursions outside. After a lot of practice, and getting used to one another, you can try making suggestions as to where to go. By this point you will have noticed that, for mainly social reasons, cats make better subjects than most other pets; you can pretty much let a cat roam at will, whereas a dog cannot be simply let loose to go where it, or you, will. Remember to take this slowly, for once an animal becomes uncomfortable they will want to shut you out, and it's almost impossible to get past these barriers. Allow at least one month of practice at each stage of the process; resting, moving around the home, moving around

outside and finally giving suggestions as to direction and purpose. As a rule of thumb, it takes about a year before a willing animal will allow you to ride with it completely.

If you do not have a pet in your home, then the process is rather more difficult in that you will need to send your astral self out in search of a willing form. This can sometimes be facilitated by putting out regular foods for wildlife and birds and making your initial acquaintance with a regular visitor. This is not to suggest that you should be catching and petting these beings, but rather that they will become accustomed to your astral presence if encouraged by your regular physical care for them. In the case of non-domesticated animals your early approaches should take the form of projecting your astral self into their vicinity rather than trying to enter their minds. Again the key is to take time on this and not to try to rush it. It can take many months to get a wild creature to become accustomed to your astral presence, let alone to allow you to ride with it.

All forms of working on the astral require a good amount of practice and perseverance. Many people find that they have to work at it regularly for months, sometimes even years, before it all seems to fall into place. Nevertheless, it is well worthwhile, as it both literally and figuratively moves your magic onto another plane. Some find that if they practise the exercises through visualization regularly enough, then the transition from the physical to the astral finally takes place without being noticed until after they return.

Dedicating yourself on the Astral

If you have not already done so you will need to create your Astral Temple, as the following Ritual is intended to take place there. You may have already been Initiated, or have performed a self-dedication in the physical realm, but it is a good idea to repeat this in your Astral Temple to mark its significance as your working space.

Travel to your Temple in your usual way, or as described above, taking all the usual precautions. Once there, arrange everything for a special and festive occasion; light any lamps or candles and perhaps include some flowers, garlands, or other decorations. Place on the Altar some of your favourite anointing oil, and in front of it a large decorative bowl full of water, and don't forget to include some wine in a chalice. Call upon the Goddess and the God to be present with you, to support, guard and guide you. When you are sure of their presence, ask them to bless and consecrate the oil from your Altar. Once this is done, add it to the water in front of the Altar. Remove all your clothing and bathe yourself from head to toe. As you do so, remember that you are washing away all the aches and pains, woes, cares and worries of the physical realm, so that you are cleansed both within and without. Once you are cleansed, anoint yourself with the oil, letting your body dry naturally in the warmth of your Temple. Dress yourself once again, in fresh clothing should you wish. If you can recall your original oath, or self-dedication, you might like to repeat this within the Temple at this time. Now take the chalice of wine and, raising it to the Goddess and the God, ask for their blessing in all your magic. Drink some and then sprinkle the remainder lightly around the edge of your Temple. When you have completed this, thank the Goddess and the God, and if you wish, remain to meditate a while. Clear and tidy your Astral Temple and return to the physical in the usual way.

Now that you have a few more skills under your belt, it is time to return to the fifth Element, and to use these skills to help you to grow closer to the Divine.

the real witches' craft

Chapter Ten

SPIRIT:

The Fifth Element

As mentioned earlier, Spirit is the fifth Element. Whilst Air, Fire, Water and Earth are the Elements of the mundane world, Spirit is the intangible and ethereal Element. It is the hardest Element to try to define, whether within or without, as you might expect from the intangible.

In the world around us Spirit is the spark of life, the difference between things living and things not. For animals and plants have their own spirit. The land itself has its own spirit, even the rocks and crystals have a form of spirit for they too grow and have a type of 'life' of their own. In us it is our inner self, the thing which makes us individual, that part of our personality which is truly ours. For we are not just the total of all that has happened to us, but we have our own essence, although this may have been affected by the events in our lives. But most importantly, Spirit is the Divine, however you perceive it. In some beliefs, that is a single Deity or God, in others it may be a number of Gods and/or Goddesses, or even an entity without gender. In yet other beliefs the Divine or Spirit is not a being or beings, being immanent; a force or energy which is present in all things.

It is equally hard to pin down the beliefs within the Craft. Most Witches believe that the Divine is both one and many, at the same time. Whilst this may seem contradictory, consider this: you too are one person and many people at the same time: To your parents you are daughter or son. To your partner you are wife, husband, girlfriend or boyfriend. If you are a parent you have yet another 'personality' to your children. If you study, there is the 'you' presented to your teachers and if you work then you may be seen as either employee or employer, boss or underling, to those you work with. Yet there is still one 'you'. Another way of looking at this could be represented by a mirror ball, many facets all reflecting different images yet only one object. For Witches, the Divine is a single whole, and yet each of the Goddesses and Gods is individual, exists apart from the others and has a 'personality', presence and existence unique and whole in their own terms. Again, for some Witches the Divine is without gender or even without form. This is why it is impossible for anyone to tell you who the Divine is, in any categorical way, and how to follow and worship it/them. It is also why it is important for you to develop your own understanding. This is one of the great freedoms of the Craft and yet one of the harder tasks of developing your magical skills. We have no paid priesthood to interpret and intercede with our Gods for us; no-one to tell us who, how and when to worship, and to dictate whether we are 'right' or 'wrong'. Nor do we have the ease and simplicity of a precise and pre-formed Divine set out for us. In the Craft we are each our own Priest or Priestess. No wonder ours has been termed 'a thinking person's belief system'.

In the Craft, the concept of the Divine is further complicated by the fact that the Goddesses and Gods are known by many names, by many different peoples, in many different places and times. Since mankind began, people have worshipped the Divine. In early times these peoples were scattered and tribal and so had different names for, and stories of, the Goddesses and Gods. Their predominant Goddesses and Gods were also often quite different; for example, a landlocked people had less connection with the Gods of the seas than their coastal 'cousins'. They interpreted their deities in the words and ways of their own lives, and passed these tales by word of mouth from one generation to another. As different peoples migrated and scattered, they took their Gods with them, and they found the same, or similar, Gods under new names. Sometimes, incoming Gods were added to the local beliefs, and sometimes newcomers would worship their own Gods but by the new names of the locality. Sometimes there were invaders who would bring their beliefs and try to overlay those of the indigenous people. As a result, there are Goddesses and Gods who merged and others who have changed. Likewise, their names, not to mention the spelling and pronunciation of them, have sometimes also altered. The stories also changed and altered, combined or diverged, although many remained the same at their core. Sometimes this resulted in new combined beliefs, or in beliefs being driven underground. So today, we have many Goddesses and Gods, even though there may be recurring themes through their stories and legends. It is from this rich history that today's Witches 'choose' their deities, although in reality it is the Gods who do the choosing!

But before you get to the stage of working with the Goddesses and Gods, it is important to start work on understanding the Spirit within, and to do this you need to have a greater understanding and acceptance of yourself. For without knowledge and understanding of yourself, how can you attempt to understand the greater Spirit? In the Craft, we do not feel that access to the Gods is only allowed to a select few, but rather that with focus and intent it is available to any. Some of the following exercises may seem, at first, unconnected to knowledge of the Goddess and the God but these are the ones which I, and other Witches I know, have tried and tested, and have found beneficial.

At first sight, 'knowing yourself' may seem obvious, but we are each a composite of our real self, our upbringing and experiences, the way we wish to appear and the way we think others expect us to be. To have true self-knowledge we need to be able to identify these separate components so that we understand each, and the place of each, in turn.

spirit: the fifth element

PRACTICAL WORK 1

Divide a sheet of paper into two columns. Head the first 'Things I like about myself', and the second 'Things I dislike about myself'. Remember you are doing this for yourself, no one else need see it, unless you leave it around. You can, and should, be completely honest! You may consider: your physical appearance; your size and shape; the colour or texture of your hair; your smile; the colour of your eyes, etc. Consider also: learned skills and talents; your abilities at cooking, typing, writing, maths, gardening, etc. List your intrinsic qualities such as: being kind to animals; being able to show sympathy; being a good judge of character; being understanding with younger people, your ability to be firm and get your own way, and so on. Because I am aware that people generally find it easier to be negative about themselves, for every item you list which is negative you really must try to find one which is positive. Don't expect to finish your lists on the first attempt, go back to them on several different days. When you feel they are complete, put them aside for three nights. After this time you can review them. Try to imagine that they are the lists from another person, so that you can be as objective as possible, or if you have a very good and trusted friend you could perhaps do the exercise together.

Look first at your list of positives and consider each item carefully. Some of these attributes will be natural, some learned or acquired. Give yourself credit for both, and note how many are things which you have deliberately changed about yourself, as in learned skills. However, be on the lookout for any which fall into the category of changes you have made to conform to others' ideas of how you should behave: it is one thing to be helpful to other people, but not at the cost of becoming a doormat. And whilst society may indicate that women should be quietly spoken, or that men should be unemotional, these are not positives if it means you are always suppressing your true character in order to conform. Obviously, I am not suggesting that you should always vent your true feelings, but that you should be aware of them.

Next, look at your list of negatives, and with careful consideration divide them into the following categories:

1. Those things which are positive, even if they may not conform to others' feelings about what is right or fashionable. For example, large feet, curly hair, a firm attitude, and so on.
2. Things which are wrong for you and which you do not need to live with, which can be changed. For example, being untidy, a fiery temper which 'goes off' in the wrong direction, not being able to cook, etc. Beside each of these, note down the changes you would like to make and keep this where you can refer to it regularly. These are things you can work on over the coming months.
3. Things which are simply a part of the real you, even if they do not fit your expectations, or those of others about how you 'ought' to be, like being short or plump, crying over weddings or sad films, etc. These are things you will need to work on accepting, rather than changing. Remember, however 'bad' you may feel they are, they are a part of the real you. As you work through this section you will almost certainly find that you share these 'failings' with one or more of the Goddesses and Gods. Not only that, but They will also have attributes which can be far worse than any you may hold.

spirit: the fifth element

The content of these categories may vary, depending on the culture of the society you live in, just as the tales of the Goddesses and the Gods do. Focus on what you know is 'right' for you, from your internal feelings; don't be influenced by anything outside, such as advertising, or the thoughts of those you live, study or work with. Learn to set aside the influences outside of you and to focus on who you truly are. This does not mean that you can or should give in to antisocial behaviour or impulses; we get along in the world by doing what we know is right and by conforming to what is acceptable in our society. However, sometimes we have to suppress our own feelings to conform and we can only be whole if we acknowledge this, even while we can still choose not to act on it. This is one of the key steps towards learning to acknowledge and understand the Divine, both inside and outside of yourself.

Some people find the above exercise quite difficult, particularly when it comes to listing their good points. This is because many of us are brought up to focus on what we do wrong, rather than on what is good about us. We are also taught that to talk about how clever or talented we are is in some way not 'nice'. Not only that, but advertising, whether in papers and magazines, or on TV or radio, is pretty much dedicated to persuading us that we will never be 'good enough' unless we purchase the products they promote! All of which makes it easier to focus on the negatives, on what we cannot do or do not have. But in order to be a balanced person we need to be comfortable with who we are, and to give ourselves credit for our positive attributes. The following exercise is one I usually give to newcomers to my Coven or group. It is also one which is well worth revisiting whenever we feel that we do not in some way measure up.

the real witches' craft

PRACTICAL WORK 2

Write a list of your good points; this should be at least 40 separate items. Once again consider physical attributes, natural talents, learned skills, and so on. The items can be as mundane as 'can make a good cup of tea', or linked to the Craft as 'have learned to read the Tarot'. Make sure you include all the things you like about yourself and those things you are good at. Review and consider those areas which may not be typically thought of as 'good', such as physical strength in a woman, or sympathy in a man. Work on this list over a period of, at the very least, a week. If you can expand the list to 100 items then you will be working along the lines I expect in my Coven. When you feel your list is complete, keep it safe so that you can look at it from time to time to remind yourself that, just like everyone else, *you* have skills and talents which are special to you.

A common side-effect when working on this list is the discovery of a number of things you would like to learn, or do. Make a note of these and identify a few, say three, that you will actually try over the next couple of months. Your Craft, and your life, can only benefit from trying new things or learning new skills.

You may have already noticed that I find list-writing a useful tool. This is because it is easy to forget a thought, especially if it is in any way uncomfortable, as honest ones often are, but it is not so easy to ignore something you have written down! However, for some people the prospect of

spirit: the fifth element

writing down their feelings is an uncomfortable one, usually because of the possibility that someone else may come across and read your inner thoughts. There are several things you can do to reduce the risk of this. The most important is not to make a big fuss about note making, or to have an obviously special book which you 'guard'. If you draw attention to what you are doing but refuse to share it with those around, you are sure to build up their curiosity. This is simply an aspect of human nature and usually a reflection of their care for you, as they want to be able to understand and, if possible, help. Another good idea is not to use an obvious diary, unless you are confident that your near and dear will respect it. Obviously, finding a safe place for your notes is important too. It is worth remembering that the easiest way to hide something is usually to put it amongst others of its kind. So if you are using an exercise book, keep it with other exercise books. One place which is least likely to be secure is the computer, especially if it is used by more than one person in your household. If you are still not happy with any of these ideas then I would still suggest that you write your lists, even if you feel that you have to dispose of them immediately. The action of writing things down is important in its own right as a way of committing things to memory. Hence, all that note-writing when studying and revising! In fact it is nearly a form of magic on its own.

Having begun work on understanding your inner self, it is also useful to look for evidence of the Divine around you. Spend time noticing the spark of life in the world. If you have pets then it can be educational to watch their behaviour. They have few social 'rules' to conform to and will usually follow their own instincts, being true to themselves. Cats are a very good example of this. In our house we currently have two adult cats and a kitten. The kitten will often want to play when her mum doesn't, and the mother cat will make this obvious. However, her father will often step in and help out, even though you can see that his heart isn't really in it. From this we can see that cats will apparently do something from a sense of 'duty', but it is equally obvious that they are aware of what they would prefer to do. Likewise, when we do the 'right' thing, which may not always be what we would prefer to do, we too should be aware of our inner feelings. We can learn much from the natural world, whether from personal observation or, if you have little contact with nature, from watching the occasional natural history programme.

The knowledge of ourselves can also be used to understand others. One of the important skills of the Witch lies in learning to know the difference between what people may say and how they really feel. Now this is not easy, as most people spend their lives learning to conceal their true feelings, with varying degrees of success. Whilst we may have a reasonably good understanding of those we are very close to, or have known for most of our lives, even their inner feelings will be hidden from us much of the time. Older people in particular will often say one thing to someone's face whilst saying something completely different once they have gone. This is not a question of being 'two-faced', but a question of the manners which they were taught when young. However, one area when feelings are almost always acted upon or discussed openly is television 'soap-land'. In order that the viewer can appreciate all the threads in the story, we get to see those feelings which in real life are not, thankfully, usually acted upon. It can be very instructive to watch the odd episode whilst considering how real people might behave in a similar situation, and indeed, what you might feel and do under similar circumstances.

Self-knowledge and understanding may seem a long way from the Goddess and the God but, as mentioned before, the Divine is the spark of life which can be found in all living things. Furthermore, Spirit being the fifth Element means that it too is both within and without, and must be understood, and in balance, to make magic work effectively. The exercises here are really only the first steps on the path to self-understanding, as this is a learning process which should continue throughout life.

Once work on the self has begun it is time to also consider the Goddess and the God outside of us. Many Witches will refer to them simply as the Goddess and the God, or the Lord and Lady, but others prefer to work with

spirit: the fifth element

them by name. Some choose different Goddesses and Gods for different forms of magic; others have preferred God-forms which they work with all, or most, of the time. Any of these approaches is equally valid, although, if you work in a group, there will have to be consensus. Obviously, it is important that, whatever your chosen Goddesses and Gods, you understand them and their stories well. Also, it is not wise to work with Goddesses and Gods from different pantheons, or groupings, at the same time, as their energies may not complement one another.

Many different pantheons of Gods have come down to us and are used in the Craft today; here are some of the most common. The Egyptian, including Isis, Osiris, Nepthys, Set and Anubis. The Greek, including Zeus, Artemis, Apollo, Hecate and Pan. The Roman, including Jupiter, Diana, Mercury, Bacchus and Juno. The Norse, including Thor, Freya, Odin, Frigg, and Loki. The Celtic, including Dagda, Morrighan, Lugh, Arianrhod and Manannan. Many of these pantheons and deities overlap, especially the Greek and Roman pantheons, so that the Greek Zeus becomes the Roman Jupiter, Artemis becomes Diana, and so on. Furthermore, there are other pantheons from all around the world.

There are two basic ways of getting to know the Gods. The first is through reading their myths and legends, and the second is through direct personal experience. However, it is better to do quite a lot of reading first, before trying to approach them. This helps you to be selective about which Gods and Goddesses you might like to work closer with. It also should give an understanding of the ways in which their roles overlap, and their tales have been subject to differing interpretations. Even if you already feel drawn to a particular pantheon or deity, it is useful to gain an understanding of others. In fact, many Witches would say that such a breadth of knowledge is essential.

PRACTICAL WORK 3

If you do not already have access to the myths and legends of the Gods at home, either in books or through the internet, then pay a visit to your local library. Any reasonable public library will have a shelf or two of books, and this can save you having to go out and spend a fortune! Have a look at several pantheons and also at different versions of the same stories. Of course, some books will be better than others, and this is in part because the style of different authors suits different people. But it is also because some authors will have put different interpretations on different stories, and some versions have been decidedly 'Christianized'.

Don't try to read everything all at once, spread your reading out so that you have time to take in a story and to consider it, before moving on to another. Think of each in terms of how it relates to the mundane world and how it might have lessons for you in your life.

When you find good or interesting reference books, make sure that you note down the title, author and reference number, so that you can find them again when you need to.

You will find some tales very interesting, whilst others may be virtually without any meaning for you. At this time, focus on the ones which appeal most; later you may find that you want to go back to the others. At some point you will come across a story, a deity or even a pantheon which appeals

to you strongly. Build on this interest by researching as much as you can. If you feel particularly drawn to a specific Goddess and/or God, try meditating on them and their story to see if you can gain further understanding of them.

Of course you should not only look to tales from foreign lands for information. Every area will have had its own local deities in the past, although finding information is often quite hard. Try looking into the origins of place names, or the names of rivers and streams. Sometimes you can get help with this from local historical societies. Local deities are important because, even though they may not be as well known as some others, they are the spirit of the land in your area. The accumulated background of their worship will give them a strength which you can directly access. This is particularly relevant when working magic for the land, whether local or in general. So however drawn you may feel to the Goddesses and Gods from elsewhere, it is important to look locally too.

As mentioned above, many of the tales we have today have been altered by translation and the passage of time, and it is useful to learn to sift through different versions to see if you can come to a better understanding of what lies beneath. For example, the standard version of the story of Persephone reads thus:

> 'Persephone, the beautiful innocent daughter of the Goddess
> Demeter, is gathering flowers in a meadow, when the earth opens
> and Pluto, God of the Dead, emerges and abducts her. He carries her
> off to Hades, the underworld, where he makes her his Queen.
> Learning from the Sun where Persephone is, her mother goes into
> mourning, allowing not a thing to grow. She takes up residence at
> Eleusis. The Gods see that no corn will sprout, and they fear that
> mankind will die, giving them no homage nor sacrifice. They appeal
> to the head of the Gods, Zeus, to intercede. Zeus commands Pluto to
> give up Persephone, but Pluto forces her to eat the seed of the
> pomegranate, thus ensuring that she will have to return to him. Zeus

the real witches' craft

decrees that Persephone must spend one third of the year in Hades
and two thirds on the surface, and so the land is fruitful for two
thirds of the year and barren for the rest.'

Seemingly, this tale is simply a way of explaining the reason why nothing grows in the winter. But there are aspects of this version which invite further investigation, not least of which is the 'black and white' nature of the story: few of the legends of the Gods are ever that straightforward. There is also the aspect that before the Christian concept of punishment after death, the Underworld was considered a kingdom in its own right, not a 'hell'. So let us consider another way of telling the same story:

'The beautiful Persephone is approaching womanhood, and like
many mothers Demeter is protective of her child. One day
Persephone wanders from home, picking flowers in a meadow.
Hades, Lord of the Underworld, drives past in his splendid chariot,
and invites Persephone to be his bride. Willingly, she goes with him.
Demeter is distraught at the disappearance of her daughter, and no
longer pays attention to her duties as Goddess of the Corn. Whilst
wandering and searching she takes work as nursemaid to the Queen
of Eleusis. One day, when collecting water from the well, Demeter
meets the Queen's daughter Baubo who lifts her skirts and exposes
herself, making the Goddess smile and causing a few shoots to rise
from the earth. The Goddess resumes her search and meets Hecate
who, as the Wise One, is able to tell her what has happened to
Persephone. Demeter travels to the underworld to seek the return of
her daughter. But as Persephone has eaten of the pomegranate
during her stay, it is necessary for her to return for a part of each
year to reign alongside Hades.'

Here we have the same tale but with a different meaning: Persephone has not been abducted, she has chosen to become the Queen of a powerful region. Demeter is not the helpless victim; she seeks and searches and even takes

spirit: the fifth element

employment in her search. When her spirits are flagging, it is the intuitive help of Baubo, another woman, which inspires her to continue. It is the Wisdom of the Crone, another aspect of the Goddess, which finally points her in the right direction. And it is Demeter herself who approaches Hades, not an intermediary. This version feels intuitively more complete. The Goddess is not dependent on male deities such as Zeus and the Sun to solve her problems for her. The tale includes all aspects of the Triple Goddess; Maiden, Mother and Crone, each linked and reliant upon the others to form a complete whole. Here the story gives much more relevant food for thought, for in it we find reflected aspects which could be a part of any woman's life: All pubescent girls find themselves seeking to move from the home of their mother to start a life of their own, and what more desirable role than that of Queen in another land? All mothers, even whilst they know this is natural and desirable, seek to put off the inevitable. But it is the Crone aspect, the wisdom of age and experience, that enables the whole to be brought to a satisfactory conclusion.

Another tale which is commonly misconstrued is that of deities Isis, Osiris, Set and Nepthys. The usual form can be briefly summarized as follows:

> 'Isis and Osiris rule Egypt but their brother Set becomes jealous and traps Osiris in a chest. Osiris escapes and so Set kills him, scattering his body across the land. Isis finds her husband's body and restores him to life. Hence, Osiris is seen as the dying and rising God, Isis as his faithful wife and healer, and Set as the evil jealous protagonist.'

Needless to say, this is not the whole story; a little research throws up some information which renders it thus:

> 'Isis, Osiris, Nepthys and Set are all the children of the great Sun God Ra. Whilst brothers and sisters, they are, as was traditional with the royal houses of Egypt, also married to one another. Ra will not share his power, or pass on his throne, so Isis creates a magical snake

*which she sends to bite him. Stricken, he sends for her to heal him
but she will not do so until he reveals his secret name. This name of
power gives her power over him. Egypt is divided into Upper and
Lower regions with Isis and Osiris governing the more profitable
region, and Nepthys and Set being given charge of the other.
Nepthys and Set become increasing jealous of their brother and sister,
not least because Set is unable to father any children. Nepthys uses
her magic to disguise herself as Isis and, creeping into his bed,
becomes pregnant by Osiris. The resulting child is Anubis. Not
surprisingly, this pushes Set over the edge of jealousy, and he devises
a way to trap Osiris. Knowing his brother's love of finery, Set creates
a lavish chest, exactly the right size for Osiris, and promises it to the
person who it fits. When Osiris claims the chest, Set seals it up with
him inside and casts it into the waters. Isis searches for and finds her
husband and restores him to her side. This time Set attacks his
brother and cuts him into thirteen pieces which are scattered across
the world. For Nepthys this is too much and she joins Isis in her
search for her husband's body. Together they recover twelve parts,
but, taking pity on her sister, Nepthys fashions an artificial phallus
and magically restores Osiris to health, that Isis might also have a
child.'*

Once again, it is the sheer simplicity of the first version which arouses some
suspicion; that and the absence of active roles for the Goddesses. As a rule of
thumb we should look more carefully at any tale which is drawn in terms of
absolute right and wrong, or totally good and wicked individuals. This is so
in life, just as it is in the legends. Consider what happens quite often when a
couple split up; people take the side of their friend, and the other person is
painted as being totally in the wrong. But the truth is usually somewhere in
the middle ground, with both parties having a level of responsibility. In the
fuller version we see that Isis and Osiris are not all good, any more than
Nepthys and Set are all bad. Each is a complex character who reacts to the
actions of the others.

spirit: the fifth element

These are just two examples of legends which bear examination; there are many more. Looking for the hidden meanings in the stories of the Goddesses and Gods is in itself an enriching experience. Not only do we increase our own knowledge but we increase our understanding of ourselves and those around us. We can also use this information to increase our awareness of how our own actions may have implications and consequences which go a lot further than many of us at first envisage, although hopefully not as far as cutting people up out of jealousy or vengeance!

PRACTICAL WORK 4

Look for a simplified version of a tale: often these can be found in books written for children, or in very simple histories. Look for inconsistencies, lack of balance and even 'christianization'. Then research the tale as thoroughly as you can, using books written for the pagan market. Now try to rewrite the story, filling it out for yourself. Don't worry about being 'historically' accurate, you are doing this as an exercise which should give you an idea of how the stories may have been interpreted and changed in the past.

There are other aspects which we should also be aware of: there are similarities across the pantheons which often come from deities being adopted by different peoples and yet the differences within those similarities can indicate where one deity has been overlaid by another. For example, the Goddess Ceres is often considered to be the Romanized version of Demeter. But they are actually different Goddesses, not versions of the same. Ceres is Roman and is the growing force of vegetation. Her festival, the fire festival of Cerealia, was celebrated in April. She was also a Goddess of the end of the harvest and the death of plants. Demeter is Greek; she is the Earth Mother and Goddess not only of the plants but also of the soil itself. The story of Ceres may have become largely submerged beneath that of Demeter, but she is nevertheless a separate divinity. Knowing the difference becomes important when working with a deity, for example, invoking Ceres to watch over your houseplants may result in them dying back at the end of the summer, rather than continuing into the next season. Thus we can see that we need to be careful of assuming that deities from different pantheons with similar stories are identical.

spirit: the fifth element

PRACTICAL WORK 5

Whilst reading stories of the Goddesses, look for references to the three aspects of Maiden, Mother and Crone, remembering that these all link to the cycles of the Moon. Not all the tales will contain these, but a good many will. Remember also that there are Goddesses of almost every aspect of life: Fertility, Growth, Fortune, Wisdom, Love, Beauty, Law, Justice, Learning, Handicrafts and many, many more. In stories of the Gods, look for his aspects of Hunter and Hunted, and roles as God of Fertility, Vegetation, Sun, War, Crafts, Wisdom, Sacrifice, and as the Horned God. Make notes of the different deities and their aspects in your journal so that you have them for later reference.

By now you will have started to gain an understanding of many different Goddesses, Gods and their pantheons, and for most people this is the point when they start to feel an affinity with one or more God forms. Now is the time to seek a more personal connection. One of the best ways to begin this is through meditation within the Circle. To prepare, you need to gather together all the information you have and create a mental image of the Goddess or God you seek to know more about. Consider their physical image, clothing, and any weapons, tools or creatures they are associated with. Try to determine which colour(s) and scents they are most often connected to. Also form an image of their surroundings and environment. If you can, create a picture or even a statue, of your chosen deity. Alternatively, see if you can find a picture or other image of them. Remember that the more effort you put into your magic, the more likely it is to be effective. Find a place for your image where you will have room to light a candle and place offerings regularly.

The following Ritual is designed to bring you closer to your chosen deity, by opening your awareness to their presence. It is best to perform it at the full Moon on the first occasion, but can be repeated on any number of occasions thereafter. Having said that, it is best to only work with one God or Goddess form in any one lunar month, to give sufficient time to develop your inner awareness; these things rarely, if ever, take place overnight!

Ritual to become closer to the Divine

In addition to your usual Altar equipment, place your picture or image in the centre of your Altar. Before it place a candle, or candles, in the colour(s) of your chosen Goddess or God, and on each side of it place one silver and one gold candle. Instead of your usual incense, use one of the appropriate scent(s). Have some salt and a shallow dish of water.

Create the Sacred Space in your usual way, lighting the silver and gold candles when you call upon the Goddess and the God. Kneel facing the image on the Altar and raise your arms above your head. Visualize the Goddess or God you would like to learn more of, and call upon them, lighting the candle before their image. In your own words ask them to come to you, to guide, guard and protect you and to bring greater insight into your life. Meditate on them for a few minutes, then perform a self-blessing in their name.

Self-Blessing

Take a pinch of salt and add it to the water, then place the forefinger of your strong hand into the water and say:

'I do bless and consecrate this in the name of the … (Goddess or God) *…* (name the Goddess or God). *May she/he likewise give their blessing to me. Blessed Be.'*

Visualize your chosen deity standing before you. Now dip your finger in the water and anoint each of your feet, saying:

'Blessed be my feet that shall follow your path. Blessed Be.'

Anoint your knees and say:

'Blessed Be my knees that shall kneel at the sacred Altar. Blessed Be.'

Anoint your pubis and say:

'Blessed be my womb (if you are female, or *loins* if you are male) *that bringeth forth the life of man. Blessed Be.'*

Anoint over your heart and say:

'Blessed be my breast that shall follow your ways. Blessed Be.'

Anoint your lips and say:

'Blessed be my lips that shall utter the sacred names. Blessed Be.'

Anoint your nose and say:

'Blessed be my nose that shall breathe the sacred essence. Blessed Be.'

Anoint your eyes and say:

'Blessed be my eyes that shall see your way. Blessed Be.'

Now wrap your arms around yourself and say:

'Bless me Mother (or 'Father' if a male deity) for I am your child. Blessed Be.'

Remain where you are for a few moments, visualizing the Goddess or the God holding you in their arms.

When you have finished, remove the Sacred Space in the usual way, and clear everything away. The image of your chosen deity and the candle before it should be placed somewhere safe where the candle can be allowed to burn all the way down.

Of course this will not give you instant understanding of your chosen deity; real knowledge only comes when you work with them on a regular basis, and then only when your intent is true and focused. Over the next lunar month continue your studies into this deity and take the time to light the occasional candle and to make regular offerings. Learn to feel how their aspects change with the phases of the Moon, and even the days of the week, as other influences come to bear. If, after a month's work, you feel that you still need to continue your search, then move on to studying another Goddess or God. Some Witches seem to know instinctively who is or are their chosen deity, or deities. For others, the search continues and indeed they may never settle on one or two but connect with whichever deity seems most appropriate at the time.

spirit: the fifth element

There are many ways of honouring your chosen deity. If you have an image, whether a picture or statue, you can light a candle or even anoint it with wine or oil on a regular basis. Some people like to keep one or two fresh flowers close by. You can dedicate work, or even chores, to them, which often has the advantage of making the work go more easily and quickly. Some Witches like to grow a plant, herb or even a tree, which they dedicate to their chosen deity. Whichever you choose, it is a good idea to try to find ways which are appropriate: Goddesses and Gods of fertility and the land are best served by offerings and work which benefit the land; those of the home by working within, or to benefit, the home, and so on.

WITCH NAMES

One of the ways some people choose to honour their chosen deity is by the taking of a name which is associated with them, often called a Witch name. Having said that, it is considered very arrogant to actually select the name of a major Goddess or God for your own. A Witch name can be the name of one of the minor deities or an aspect of a deity. It could be the name of an historical figure, perhaps significant within the Craft. It could come from nature and be the name of an animal, bird, herb, plant or tree. It can even be a place. Such names can be actual, historical or even fictional.

It is sometimes said that Witch names were used to protect the identities of the Witches of the past from discovery, although I find this unlikely as it indicates that people who lived within a locality would not have been already known to one another by sight. Certainly today, such names are most often chosen to mark the 'rebirth' into the Craft, and occasionally to protect a person's identity if they work in a sensitive area. A Witch name is not the same as a pen-name, which may be used by an author, or on the internet.

There are many ways of selecting a Witch name. You may find there is a name which just comes to you. You may come across one in the course of your study of the Craft. If you work within a formal Coven then it may be chosen for you. The name may be associated with your chosen deity, or completely unrelated. There are, however, some things to be aware of when selecting a name, as it is supposed to stay with you for the rest of your life. Research the name carefully; it may have associations which you do not want to take on yourself; for example, Deirdre, who was renowned for her beauty but was also known as Deirdre of the Sorrows because grief and disaster came to those she loved. It is also best to select something which you can not only pronounce but also spell! And try to avoid names with unintentional puns, or which are over-long and flowery, as they tend to be treated with a certain amount of humour!

In Coven life a Witch name is usually taken, or given at the second degree, but Solitaries will often take theirs at the time they self-dedicate. That said, it is perfectly acceptable to take a Witch name at any time, or indeed not to take one at all.

Getting to know your personal deity or deities gives a very real sense of purpose to working in the Craft and brings a sharper, more effective focus to all magical working. Knowledge of their stories and mythology can also bring a greater understanding of the natural rhythms which rule and structure our lives.

spirit: the fifth element

Chapter Eleven

MAGICAL TIMING

As Witches, we seek to live in tune with the land and its natural cycles; the seasons of the year, the phases of the Moon, the flow of the tides, the movements of the stars, and even day and night. All these have their own natural energies which wax and wane, ebb and flow, and which are linked to each other. For example, the waxing and waning of the Moon and the seasons of the year contribute directly to the rise and fall of the tides, which is why a full Moon which coincides with the Spring Equinox means that the tides at such a time will be higher than usual.

Scientifically, this is explained through the variations in orbit of the Earth around the Sun, and the Moon around the Earth, and the fluctuations in gravitational pull caused by this. Likewise, but to a lesser extent, the movements of the other planets also produce disturbances in the energy flows of the Solar system. It is not surprising that the energies which influence the waters of our planet also influence us, the people who live upon it; after all we are mainly comprised of water. Indeed, it is well known that people have cycles which are linked to the lunar phases, the most obvious being the menstrual cycle. But it is not just the fluctuations in hormones which cause variations in the energy levels and temperament of women of child-bearing age. There are cycles of mood, intellect, energy, inspiration and so on, also mirroring the lunar month, which can be found, to a greater or lesser extent in all people. These variations of mood and energy have an impact not only on the individual and give us times when magic is easier or harder, but also on the external energies which make it easier or harder to work differing types of spell or magic.

magical timing

PRACTICAL WORK 1

If you are not already doing so, keep a diary into which you make a note of your feelings and energy levels. Make notes on your physical, mental and emotional energy levels, together with the day and date, phase of the Moon, and the stage of the season. It is worth being fairly detailed about both lunar and seasonal information, for example writing New Moon plus three days, rather than just noting whether it is waxing or waning. Try to make a point of actually looking at the Moon every night, rather than just taking the information from an almanac or calendar. Even better, try to go outside to look at it, and note where in the sky it both rises and sets. Likewise, note the season in terms of what is actually appearing in nature, rather than just 'early spring'. Also, note down any other external factors which may affect your energy levels, as obviously a couple of days of disturbed sleep, for example, will leave all your energy levels at a low. You may also be able to find some of this information from the earlier diaries you wrote from other exercises in this book. For this diary to be really useful, you will need to keep it for at least several months and preferably a whole year. But it is really worthwhile if you want to be able to fine-tune not only your magic, but other areas of life which are affected by energy levels.

It's worth mentioning that the timing of any piece of magic to season or lunar phase is not critical, otherwise you could be waiting a long time to be able to work some spells, but that the more of these energy tides you can tap into, the easier it becomes to work really effective magic.

the real witches' craft

PHASES OF THE MOON

In the Craft the most commonly used, and known, energy tides are those of the Moon. I appreciate that most of my readers will already be aware of the influences of the phases of the Moon and the ways these can be harnessed in magical working, but for those who aren't, and for the sake of completeness I will include them here, hopefully giving some fresh insights for more experienced readers too. The Moon has a cycle lasting a little over twenty-nine days, which consists of: new Moon, waxing (increasing) Moon, full Moon, waning Moon, and Dark of the Moon. During the waxing phase it passes through the first quarter and during the waning phase it passes through the third quarter, both of which are seen in the sky as what are called, somewhat confusingly, half Moons. Broadly speaking, the new and waxing Moon are seen as a time for working magic to draw things toward you, and the waning Moon for sending things away. But it is worth looking at the whole cycle in more detail. Here I shall refer to nights of the Moon, as this is generally the time that the Moon is most easily seen, but it is worth remembering that the Moon can sometimes be seen during the day and that, seen or not, it is still in its phase.

- *The new Moon* is deemed to be the three nights starting with the first sliver of Moon in the sky. This part of the cycle is a good time for magic related to new ideas, new starts and fresh beginnings. Work spells at this time for inspiration, and to help in determining which direction to go. It is also the time for working spells which are expected to have long-term effects or to be slow in starting, and delayed action spells.
- *The first quarter* of the Moon is the four to five nights following the new, up to the half-Moon mark. It looks like a steadily thickening reverse C in the sky. Work spells at this time which draw things towards you, such as new friends, opportunities, increased energy. Also for spells related to employment and earnings.
- *The second quarter* runs from the half Moon to the night before the full Moon. This is the best time for spells seeking growth and increase. Work

magical timing

magic to develop your knowledge and understanding, and for help in any studies or new projects you have undertaken.

- *The full Moon*, like the new, is deemed to last for three nights. This is the time when the energy makes the change from waxing to waning, and is a good time for all forms of divination. Work for partnerships and consolidation. This is also the time to give thanks to the Goddess and the God, not just for the spells you may be working, but for all the things they have brought into your life.

- *The third quarter* lasts from the day after the full up to the next half Moon. This time is good for working all spells of protection and defence. For reinforcing barriers and boundaries, for clearing out and for sorting things through.

- *The fourth quarter* runs from the last half Moon to the point at which it ceases to show in the sky, three nights before the new Moon, and looks like a decreasing C in the sky. Use this phase for banishing and driving things away like negative thoughts and energies, and to remove things like bad habits.

- *The Dark of the Moon* is the three nights when no Moon is visible at all. In your earlier days in the Craft you may well have been advised not to work any magic at this time. This is because the energies of this period can be very uncertain and, for those who work in Covens, it helps to avoid the Elders needing to spend a lot of time undoing rash and ill-advised spells which have gone wrong! As the energies can be so fickle, always use divination to ascertain the potential results of any spells which you feel you must work at this time, or work in your Astral Temple, changing the phase to one which is better suited to your spell.

It helps if you also remember that the phases of the Moon are linked to the aspects of the Goddess: the new and waxing reflecting the Maiden, the Full as the Mother, and the waning Moon as the Crone or Wise One.

In the above I have made no mention of healing magics, because healing in particular can be undertaken at any of the phases, as you can temper the spell to reflect the phase. For example, attracting healing strength and energy in the early part of the cycle, or the banishing of illness in the latter.

TIDAL RHYTHMS

As mentioned above, the tides are influenced by the action of the Moon. Tides ebb and flow daily, or twice daily in some areas. Unless you live very close to the sea you may well be unaware of the tides, but this can easily be rectified by purchasing a table of tides for the part of the coast closest to your home; these are usually relatively inexpensive. If you have strong connections with the sea in another place, perhaps the home of your family, or somewhere with which you have a spiritual connection, then it may be worth getting a copy of these too. There are basically two stages of tidal movement: ebb and flow. Between each there is a point of stasis, when the tide is neither 'going out' nor 'coming in'. The ebb tide, when the water moves away from the land, is the time of sending things away, whilst the flow is for drawing things towards you.

If you are able to actually go to the coast then working at the water's edge can be very effective: Spells on the flow can be inscribed into the sand at low tide so that the incoming sea takes them. At the ebb, spells can be inscribed onto thin paper which is torn up and scattered onto the outgoing waters. Investigating the water line, especially after a storm, can often reveal many gifts of nature which can be taken home for use in spell work. Look for stones, pebbles, shells and interestingly shaped driftwood.

SEASONS

We are all aware that the different seasons of the year can affect the way we feel. In the summer we feel more alert and aware, and in the winter more inclined to spend time in passive pursuits. If you have any doubts about these

magical timing

effects then you only have to experience jet lag, or erratic shift-work, to appreciate how closely our physical and mental functions are linked to a regular daylight cycle, and the same is true over longer periods of time. In the summer we feel more energetic and alert, and inclined to spend time outside; in the winter our thoughts turn to warming foods, and staying indoors. This is in part because of the changing weather, but mostly because of the changes in the length of daylight. Our natural body rhythms have been adapting for millennia to the cycles of the Sun. Likewise, the seasons have their own magical energies, to which our abilities have become in tune, if only we listen.

PRACTICAL WORK 2

Take a sheet of paper for each of the seasons of spring, summer, autumn and winter, and on it write all the things you feel relate to each season. These might include the signs of the season; weather, plant growth, animal life, etc. Also include your preferred activities and/or sports, chores or tasks, more abstract associations such as colours, scents, and so on. Make your lists as complete as you can, even if you feel that some of your associations are a bit tenuous. Put the list to one side for a day or two and then review it and add the sorts of spell you feel might be most appropriate to each season. It might be best if you do this before reading on, so that you can compare your thoughts with those which follow.

You may have noticed, as you went through the above exercise, that you have different preferences and inclinations from one season to another, even though you rarely get the chance to follow them. Our lives today are so restricted by the need to earn a living and fit in with the world around us that we have lost the option of living in a seasonal manner. Even if you are part of a farming community the seasons will have become blurred by the introduction of year-round farming techniques; varieties of crops, fertilizers, chemicals, etc all intended to maximize land use. But in the Craft we can find both the time and the way to stay in tune with these seasonal flows.

It's worth remembering that the seasons are not discreet events, they blend into one another, and, contrary to the rest of our over-scheduled lives, do not

begin and end on fixed dates. Whilst some people work on the assumption that the equinoxes and solstices fall in the middle of their seasons, in fact these more closely mark the beginning of each. Even with global warming, no one would suggest that summer is at its height in the middle of June. And of course in the southern hemisphere, the seasons are reversed.

- *Spring* is the time of growth, with plants emerging from their winter's rest and animals beginning a new cycle of pairing and breeding. This is a time of beginnings, of inspiration and optimism. Remember how your mood lifts on the first noticeably warmer and sunnier days? It is also a time of renewed energy. This is a good time for spells for renewal and new growth, for starting new projects and seeking new directions.
- *Summer* is the time of ripening, of longer days and shorter nights. Fruits and grains grow and young animals learn independence. Despite, or more likely because of, the longer days and greater warmth, this is not a time of great energy, but rather a time of development and consolidation. Spells for growth and development work well at this time. Work for harmony and understanding within the circle of your friends and family.
- *Autumn* brings shortening daylight hours, fruition and harvest. It is a time of rewards and celebration. Like spring there is more energy at this time, but of a different kind. This is a season of preparation for the rigours to come. This is a time for correcting mistakes and errors; for putting things to rights.
- *Winter* is the season of rest and withdrawal. This is the time of reflection and of turning inwards. Our thoughts are more often of our hearth and home, and of our near and dear. These energies can be used to enhance aspects of review, rethinking and renewal. Carry out self-assessment and work divination, to determine your direction for the year ahead. Work magic to help those around you to make the best choices and decisions.

Whilst there are not very many spells which can wait for the 'right' season, seasonal influences can be harnessed for the more long-term life-changing magics we want to work. We can also use the energies of each season to

the real witches' craft

empower our magic if we design the spell with these energies in mind, perhaps by putting the emphasis of the spell onto the aspect most suited to the season. Of course, if you work in your Astral Temple then you can work in the season there most suited to your magic, regardless of the season on the physical plane.

SABBATS

The Sabbats are our seasonal festivals and in your earlier study of the Craft you may well have been advised that they were times of celebration, rather than for the working of magic. However, there are strong energies connected to the Sabbats which can also be incorporated in our spells and magic. Having said that, many Witches prefer to keep their Sabbats as times of renewal and reflection; only working magic at them when it is really essential.

The Sabbats are divided into two groups: the major Sabbats of Samhain, Imbolg, Beltane and Lughnasadh, and the minor ones which are the Spring and Autumn Equinoxes and the Winter and Summer Solstices. The former are linked to the agricultural cycle and would originally have been timed by events in nature. Later they were assigned dates, but as these were in the old calendar, they would have fallen some eleven days earlier than the ones we now use. The latter are associated with the movements of the Earth around the Sun and, whilst they have been given 'set' dates, which I've included for the sake of completeness, if you intend to use them for magical purposes it is better to seek their actual timing.

- *Samhain* 31 October. This festival marks the beginning of the fogs, frosts and storms which herald the onset of winter. The harvest is gathered and stocks put aside for the resting part of the year. At this time the Goddess takes on her robes as the Crone and the God takes his place as leader of the Wild Hunt. Traditionally, this is a time for the resting and renewal of the land, and for divination. As the festival of the dead, it is also the time

magical timing

for remembering those who have gone before. Magically, it is the time for reassessment and for looking to the future. Use the energies in spells where you seek guidance for new directions, or for reviewing life plans. This is also a good time for spells of defence and protection.

⚘ *Yule* 21 December. The winter Solstice, this marks the moment when the days begin to lengthen, and the nights to shorten again. It is the time of the rebirth of the Sun. Whilst in many parts of the northern hemisphere the temperature is still dropping, this is nevertheless a time of reborn hope and optimism. The energies of this festival can be used in magic for changing entrenched habits and attitudes. A remnant of this can be seen in the New Year's resolutions which are made today.

⚘ *Imbolg* 2 February. This is the time of the first signs of the new growth of spring, snowdrops appear and the first lambs are born. At this time the Goddess changes her robes to those of the Maiden. The energies of this season are those of birth and renewal, so use them in fertility and conception spells.

⚘ *Oestara* 21 March. The Spring Equinox, this is the day when day and night are of equal length. It is also the festival of the Goddess Eostar, a form of Astarte, whose emblems are the hare and the egg of rebirth. Oestara is the time of casting off the old and taking on the new, hence our modern tradition of spring cleaning. Traditionally, we use the energies of this festival for clearing out on the mental and emotional levels, to cast off old habits and doubts and to rid ourselves of unnecessary guilts, and to take on new ways of thought and new aspirations.

⚘ *Beltane* 1 May. Here we have the signs of the onset of summer, and this festival was traditionally marked by the blossoming of the Hawthorne. This is also the festival where the Goddess takes on her robes of the Mother, and of the marriage of the Goddess and the God. This festival has long been used as the time for Handfasting, and for the renewal and strengthening of relationships. Use its energies to enhance all ties with loved ones, whether romantic or otherwise.

the real witches' craft

- *Litha* 21 June. The Summer Solstice, this marks the moment when the lengthening days and shortening nights give way to shortening days and lengthening nights. The height of the Sun's energy can be used in spells for energy, vitality and renewal, and to reinforce long-term spells for health and prosperity.

- *Lughnasadh* 1 August. The festival of the Celtic God Lugh and the first of the harvest. Lughnasadh, or Lammas as it is also known, is marked by the first cutting of the ripened corn. Traditionally, this is a festival of sacrifice, with blood and wine being given back to the land in payment for the coming of the harvest. The energies of this festival can be used in magic for growth and development, for recognition, progress and advancement.

- *Madron* 21 September. The Autumn Equinox, this is once again the time when day and night are equal, and hence another time of balance. This time the emphasis is on thanks and repayment, rather than on clearing out and starting anew. In keeping with the balance of the season, the energies can be used for magic working on inner balance. It is a time for preparing for the dark months of the winter's season by ensuring that debts are paid, both literally and spiritually.

Even if you do decide to use the Sabbat energies in your magic and spells it is also worth making a point of using them as times of reflection on the passage of the seasons and on each festival's place in the Wheel of the Year.

magical timing

PRACTICAL WORK 3

In your journal put aside a page for each of the Sabbats and on it write down your thoughts and feelings on each. It can help if you deal with one at a time, perhaps on separate days. Start by meditating on each, perhaps looking back through your own records and remembering what you have done at each in the past. Try to build up your own picture of the energies of the festival, both in terms of how you felt and in terms of how the world around you appeared to be changed. Keep these pages to one side so that you can add to them as you go through the cycle of the coming year. Pick, as your starting point, the Sabbat closest to the point in the Wheel where you are reading this.

DAYS OF THE WEEK

Each day of the week has its own energies. They are linked to the inner planets and also have Gods and Goddesses associated with them.

- *Monday* – The Moon rules over the feminine principle and female fertility. Its energy can be used to order the emotions, and to bring them under personal control. It is also useful for divination, review of the past, the removal of illusion and all aspects of uncovering the truth of a matter.

- *Tuesday* – Mars is the planet of conflict and defence. Use its energy to bring courage, resolve conflicts, control impulsiveness and to strengthen resolution, and also for all acts of defensive magic. As it also orders physical sexuality, be careful to use its energy wisely.

the real witches' craft

- *Wednesday* – Mercury is the planet of communication. Its energy can be used to enhance all spells for thought, knowledge, and the intellect. Also for magic associated with travel and distance.
- *Thursday* – Jupiter rules over hope, luck, fate and wealth. Use its energy to bring success in ventures related to careers and material prosperity.
- *Friday* – Venus is the planet of friendship, romance and love. Use its energy in all self-help spells as well as to increase bonds with friends and family. It also brings success in artistic ventures and encourages artistic creativity.
- *Saturday* – Saturn is the planet of wisdom, excellence and status. It enhances self-control, the ability to bring order to confusion, and can be used to strengthen resolve. Its energies can also be brought to strengthen binding and banishing.
- *Sunday* – The Sun rules over the masculine principle and male fertility. Its energy can be used to reinforce the will, to assert identity, and to bring strength to the ego. Use it also to bring extra energy to spells and vitality to life in general. Its influence also helps in scientific pursuits.

magical timing

PRACTICAL WORK 4

Look back to the diaries you have been keeping as you have worked through this book, and any other journals you may have kept. See if you can identify any patterns in the energies around you which you feel link to the days of the week. Also look to see if your energy levels vary on a daily basis.

Many people find that they have a weekly cycle with some days being better for some aspects of their lives than others, aside from the common dislike of Monday mornings of course!

If you can, find out which day of the week you were born on. Many people find that this is the day when their personal energy is strongest, so that their magic will work best if attuned to this day.

Of course, the cycle of day and night also has an effect on people and their energies, although generally speaking most Witches find that their energies are higher when the Moon is visible, which is nearly always during the hours of darkness. However, it is worth looking at whether you are, by inclination, a day or a night person. And this is not just as simple as whether you like to rise with the Sun or not. These days very few of us get the chance to wake and sleep in what would be our natural rhythm, or for that matter to eat when we actually need to, rather than on a pre-determined schedule. It you do have the opportunity it can be quite enlightening to find your own natural rhythm, but as it takes at least a month of continuously being able to follow your own cycle without external constraints I feel it's not a useful exercise to include here. However, you might find it useful to monitor, in a more casual way, the variations in your energy levels over the daylight and night-time hours over a short period of time. This has the advantage of giving you information which is relevant to the lifestyle you actually lead rather than your natural, but less easily achievable, rhythm.

PLANETARY HOURS

Just as the different days and nights have their own energies so do the hours within the days. However, these are not the regulated hours of sixty minutes, but rather 'hours' which are comprised of equal segments of day and night. Thus, despite the varying length of daylight there is the same number of hours, whilst their duration, in minutes, will vary.

When calculating planetary hours you need to know the times of sunrise and sunset, so that you can determine the length of day and night. Each is then divided into twelve hours. Thus in winter the daytime planetary hours are shorter and those at night longer, and vice versa in the summer.

The hours are always assigned in the same sequence; Sun, Venus, Mercury, Moon, Saturn, Jupiter, Mars. Each day's hours start with the first daylight hour being assigned the planet associated with that: Monday with Moon, Tuesday with Mars, Wednesday with Mercury, Thursday with Jupiter, Friday with Venus, Saturday with Saturn and Sunday with the Sun. And the sequence continues through the day and night giving:

Monday daylight: Moon, Saturn, Jupiter, Mars, Sun, Venus, Mercury, Moon, Saturn, Jupiter, Mars, Sun.

Monday night: Venus, Mercury, Moon, Saturn, Jupiter, Mars, Sun, Venus, Mercury, Moon, Saturn, Jupiter.

magical timing

Tuesday daylight: Mars, Sun, Venus, Mercury, Moon, Saturn, Jupiter, Mars, Sun, Venus, Mercury, Moon.

Tuesday night: Saturn, Jupiter, Mars, Sun, Venus, Mercury, Moon, Saturn, Jupiter, Mars, Sun, Venus.

Wednesday daylight: Mercury, Moon, Saturn, Jupiter, Mars, Sun, Venus, Mercury, Moon, Saturn, Jupiter, Mars.

Wednesday night: Sun, Venus, Mercury, Moon, Saturn, Jupiter, Mars, Sun, Venus, Mercury, Moon, Saturn.

Thursday daylight: Jupiter, Mars, Sun, Venus, Mercury, Moon, Saturn, Jupiter, Mars, Sun, Venus, Mercury.

Thursday night: Moon, Saturn, Jupiter, Mars, Sun, Venus, Mercury, Moon, Saturn, Jupiter, Mars, Sun.

Friday daylight: Venus, Mercury, Moon, Saturn, Jupiter, Mars, Sun, Venus, Mercury, Moon, Saturn, Jupiter.

Friday night: Mars, Sun, Venus, Mercury, Moon, Saturn, Jupiter, Mars, Sun, Venus, Mercury, Moon.

Saturday daylight: Saturn, Jupiter, Mars, Sun, Venus, Mercury, Moon, Saturn, Jupiter, Mars, Sun, Venus.

Saturday night: Mercury, Moon, Saturn, Jupiter, Mars, Sun, Venus, Mercury, Moon, Saturn, Jupiter, Mars.

Sunday daylight: Sun, Venus, Mercury, Moon, Saturn, Jupiter, Mars, Sun, Venus, Mercury, Moon, Saturn.

Sunday night: Jupiter, Mars, Sun, Venus, Mercury, Moon, Saturn, Jupiter, Mars, Sun, Venus, Mercury.

Use of the planetary hours gives another way of enhancing your magic. If you want to use the energies of the Sun you can increase the effect of working on a Sunday by using one of the planetary hours linked to the Sun. Alternatively, if your spell cannot wait several days, then you could work on any day but use the hour associated with the influence you seek. If you feel that you are likely to use planetary hours often, then it might be a good idea to put the above into a table for ease of reference.

OTHER PLANETARY INFLUENCES

Astrology is another way of calculating planetary influences as it calculates their position and uses their proximity to the Earth to determine the level of their energy. It also includes the outer planets, although as they are much further away, and their orbits are far longer, their effects are more subtle. It is far too large a subject to cover here. But, as you are no doubt aware, the different planets, many of which we looked at in the Daily energies, move around the Sun and are therefore at different distances from the Earth at different times. When a planet is close its influence will be greater than if it is further away. Their orbits vary in size and hence in duration, which means that calculating their position with any degree of accuracy is something of a mammoth task. Fortunately, there are tables, and even computer programs which simplify the task. However, even for a dedicated astrologer it is still quite complex to determine when would be the best time for any particular spell. It requires calculating the positions of the most efficacious planets, and any which might overrule them, over a period of time to determine the best date and time for the spell. Although computerized astrology programs make

magical timing

this easier, it still takes some time to do this accurately. Furthermore, you may find that the best aspected date is not for several months. For these reasons most Witches will use planetary hours rather than astrology.

As mentioned earlier, spells and magic can rarely wait until the time is 'right', let alone until all the above have fallen into line. However, all these different energies do have an impact on magical working and if you can use one or more of the energies the easier you will find it. As an analogy, consider rowing a boat along a river from A to B. If the boat is empty, you row in the direction of the current, and the wind is in your favour, then the journey will be easy. But if you have to travel against both wind and water, and the boat is laden, then whilst you will still get there, it will require a great deal more energy. As you become more proficient, you will also be able to incorporate the energies of timing into your astral workings. But whilst we are still learning and growing, probably the most important thing is to learn how to protect and to defend ourselves.

Chapter Twelve

THE DARKER
SIDE OF MAGIC

This chapter, as the title implies, is about those aspects of the Craft which relate to putting things right. It's about protection and defence; not only on the astral, which was mentioned earlier, but also in our magical working lives. It's also about dealing with negative magics: hexes, curses and the like, and with spells that go wrong.

It would be nice to think that the whole of the Craft is just about healing and improving the lives of those we love, not to mention our own. However, life is not quite like this, and as a result we also need to learn to protect ourselves and defend those we love. This is not because, as is sometimes supposed, the world is full of individuals who spend their time creating hexes and curses designed to destroy us. Nor is it because life is teeming with unpleasant entities which are determined to take us over; another common misconception. But rather, it is more likely to be because there are negative energies and influences which can have an impact on us. Think of it this way: you have no need to expect the attacks of some form of super-mage who zaps your life with their magic, or the appearance of gruesome hell-fiends, both of which are so beloved of TV and the movies. What you may find is that your life can be affected by the sort of negative energies which cause more mundane happenings, more like the feeling that you're having a run of bad luck.

DEFENDING YOURSELF AGAINST NEGATIVITY

Negative energies can come from all around; they need not be actually directed at us personally to feel the impact of them. You will almost certainly be aware of the feeling you get when you come across a couple of people who have been arguing; negativity hangs in the air. You may also have found that this has an effect on you; perhaps you knock into a piece of furniture, or forget what you are about to say. This is a fairly low level of negativity, and stronger effects will be noticed in ongoing disputes, or where there is long-term resentment, such as in a boundary dispute between neighbours. Any kind of general negativity happening around you can have knock-on effects in your life, unless you have protected yourself. Of course, if you have really upset and offended someone, then you could well be the subject of their deliberate negative thoughts, although this does not mean they are in any way working magic against you. Negativity can also accumulate, so that the long-term results of a period of minor problems may actually be worse than the most recent difficulty you can recall. This is why we keep our magical defences well maintained, both our own and those around the people and things which are important to us.

Whilst you can, of course, do this simply by creating and regularly renewing your defences, it is also useful to actually check to see if it is present. For some, negativity can be seen as a sort of grey mist or fog, with tendrils, but it can also take other forms. Sometimes it is easier to detect if you view your home from the astral.

the real witches' craft

PRACTICAL WORK 1

Defend yourself in the usual way, and project yourself out of your body. Visit each room in your home in turn and examine it thoroughly. Look into cupboards and under beds and so forth. When you have finished with the inside, also check it from the outside; look carefully at all the windows and doors. Sometimes you may find tendrils of negativity clinging to the outside, either looking for a way in, or if there is a lot of negativity, overflowing from the inside. If there are any outbuildings, such as a garage, check these too. Likewise, if you have a car, or other means of transport, look at this. Once you have completed your tour of inspection, return to yourself and make a note of the places in which you detected any form of negativity and your feelings, if any, on what it might relate to.

You will almost certainly find that negativity accumulates in the same sort of places where you might expect to find cobwebs and dust-balls. This is because it finds it easier to exist in out of the way and forgotten places. In fact dirt, dust and fluff actually attract negativity. For this reason, it is a good idea to keep your home clean and tidy. Even if you are one of those people who like to encourage spiders, you should still remove old dusty webs; after all, the spider will have long moved on as it too prefers a clean home! Also open the windows as often as you can to allow a through-flow of air, as sunlight and fresh air help to prevent negative energies gaining a hold.

the darker side of magic

If you have a big build-up of negativity, or are moving into a new home, it is a good idea to perform a full magical cleansing (after ensuring all is clean and tidy). If you can, open all the doors and windows, but if the weather's too inclement then work from room to room, closing them as you go. Using a besom, or broomstick, sweep each room deosil (clockwise), from the centre outwards, finishing at the open window or door. As you do so, visualize all the negativity being swept away. Make sure you include the whole room, moving as much of the furniture as you can to get under or behind it. If this is truly impossible, then you will have to use your visualization skills to extend the use of the besom into these areas. This is the cleansing. It is a good idea to follow this with some basic protection: Using an Asperger, and still moving deosil, cast a light sprinkling of salt and water around each room, whilst visualizing it as a wall of defence around each room as well as the whole house.

PRACTICAL WORK 2 — CREATING A BARRIER OF PROTECTION ON THE ASTRAL

Most Witches will create an astral barrier around their homes, and renew it regularly, usually monthly. The area protected will include the whole of the home, including the garden and any transport. This not a form of paranoia, but rather the feeling of better safe than sorry. This form of protection can also be applied to the homes of your loved ones if they live elsewhere. For most Witches this is done using visualization, although some will also perform the same ritual in the physical world as well. It is usually preceded by cleansing on the astral, even if this has been recently done.

Taking the usual precautions, allow yourself to move out of your body. Once on the astral, take a besom and sweep through the whole of your home, in the way described above, although being on the astral you will be able to move through the walls and floors of your home to include the land under and the space above, so that you complete a sphere. Then call upon the Element of Air to blow through the whole, removing all traces of negativity, and thank it once it has done so. Repeat with Fire, asking it to burn away all negativity, and then with Water to wash it away. With the Element of Earth, call upon the very fabric of the land, and the bricks and stones, etc of the building to actually repel it. Then walk the boundary of the property deosil, sprinkling iron filings and salt as you go. Once you have completed the circuit, overlapping the ends to ensure there are no gaps, empower the boundary of iron and salt

the darker side of magic

to rise up and complete the sphere of protection and defence. Lastly, call upon the Goddess and God to consecrate this sphere, and to add their energy to the protection of your home and all that you hold dear.

Although the above is more than sufficient, there are other traditional methods which you could also use. Placing small pieces of mirror, the kind used for tiling in bathrooms are best, facing outwards in each window, will deflect all kinds of negativity, even if it has been intentionally focused your way. And it used to be common to see a glass ball, the kind known as a fisherman's float, hanging in the window, which also has the effect of deflecting negativity. There are also a large number of herbs, trees and plants which can be grown around the house for protection. These include Angelica, Basil, Geranium, Lavender, Rosemary, Violet and Yew, to name but a few.

You may also find that negativity clings around, or to, certain objects, and it is worth considering the history of these. For example, it will certainly be attracted to anything which was a present from an ex-partner with whom you had an acrimonious break-up and, whilst you can try cleansing, it is often better not to hang on to such things. Likewise, anything which you have acquired second-hand may contain traces of negativity which can usually be removed by magical cleansing. This can be performed by placing it in the light of the full Moon for three nights, or by holding it under running water, both of which will usually suffice. If, however, you feel that the object is not sufficiently cleansed in this way, then you may need to consider whether you should in fact keep this thing. At one time it used to be fairly common for Witches to use a bayonet blade in their Athame, and many of these were bought second-hand. Whilst this worked well in cases where the blade had never been used, some people found that theirs contained such strong feelings of negativity that they were obliged to get rid of them. If the object really is something you can't bear to part with, then you can try cleansing it through the Elements and performing a banishing of unwanted influences. Create your Sacred Space in the usual way, with the Elements actually in place on the Altar. Pass the object through each of them in turn, calling upon them to drive out all negativity and to cleanse it with their respective powers of wind, flame, water and the absorption of earth. Then place your object onto the Altar and call upon the Goddess and God to bless it. Whilst you work you will need to observe the object with your sixth sense, so that you can actually see when each Element has achieved its purpose, and lastly until you observe both the Goddess and the God give their blessings.

Just occasionally you may come across someone who seems to trail negativity around as they go. I'm not thinking of someone who is just going through a bad patch and may be feeling a bit down, but the sort of person who leaves those they meet with a generally negative feeling, even though the person may seem to be quite positive enough. Sometimes these individuals also seem to drain all your energy whenever you meet them, and spending any length of time in their presence becomes exhausting, no matter how much you enjoy their company. It is always worth considering whether this is your sixth sense telling you to be careful, or the inner-you feels that this person may cause you harm or hurt in some way. And it is always worth paying attention to these sorts of inner feelings as they are frequently correct. However, you may not be able to stay away from this person, possibly they are a co-worker or your employer.

There are also some people who generate this sort of feeling, who are otherwise quite benign. They are often referred to as being 'psychic vampires'. This does not mean that they suck your blood, but rather that they seem to feed off your psychic, or even physical, energy. Most psychic vampires are quite unaware of the effect they have, and would be very upset if you were to suggest such a thing, as it seems to be just a facet of their personality. If you know someone like this then it is worth taking extra steps to protect yourself whenever you are likely to come into contact with them. And if they are friends, then it's worth doing so discreetly! The simplest way of doing this is to activate your circle within, and to keep it in place until you leave their company. You could also empower an amulet for protection, by placing a protective circle within this which you can then activate to surround you.

The above protections will, if performed and used properly, normally be more than sufficient to keep you safe and secure. They are not, however, a cure-all and won't prevent the normal ups and downs of life. It's important to remember that whilst the Craft is worthwhile and beneficial, it does not mean you'll lead a charmed life from now on! So sometimes you may need to take further steps to protect yourself and those you care for.

I am often asked, usually by sceptics who are convinced Witchcraft must be evil, if the 'power' we talk about using in our spells can be used for ill as well as for good. The short answer is 'yes' it can but, as Witches, we observe the Wiccan Rede which states, 'An it harm none, do what you will.' We are also aware of the Law of Three-fold Return which says that whatever you do, good or ill, will be returned three times over. Also there is a great risk in working negative spells; if the person you direct them towards has even an iota of magical ability they will be able, relatively easily, to turn your spell back on you. Not only that, but working negative magic has the effect of reducing the worker's ability to work any kind of magic at all.

Having said that, it is just possible that you may come across someone who feels that the potential results are worth the risks. This is extremely rare, thankfully, but it can happen. Now, obviously, the first step towards dealing with this is prevention. Logically speaking, if you don't go around upsetting people, they will hardly want to take any risks by working negative magic against you! However, life in general, and some people in particular, cannot be relied upon to act logically, so we need to know how to protect ourselves should it become necessary.

So what do you do if you suspect that negative magic is being used against you? And how do you counter it? Well, negative magic, like general negativity, usually manifests itself in things going wrong in life. Not just the ordinary ups and downs of daily existence, but things which cannot be easily explained. For example, eggs, milk and the like may go off far sooner than usual, or several electrical appliances go wrong within a day or so of each other. There may be more rows and arguments than usual, or things get broken, lost or misplaced more than normal. These are often accompanied by the onset of illness, sleeplessness, bad dreams and general malaise. The effects may be felt by more than one member of the household, including pets. If your psychic sense is attuned, you will also notice a change in the atmosphere of the home, and the onset of the sort of fogginess that negativity brings with it.

Having noticed one or more indicators of negative magic, the best thing to do is to repeat the first exercise in this chapter, being particularly aware of negativity entering, or trying to enter the home. It is important that you do this in your own home, then you will be able to detect the magic whether it is being directed at you personally, or at your household. If you are in another location, then obviously you will only be able to detect that which is directed at you.

Assuming your home is already cleansed and protected, it will be easy to spot any negativity being directed towards you. Make a point of looking for the direction it is coming from as this can help you to track down the sender. It's worth bearing in mind that magical practitioners, whether Witches or otherwise, are not going to waste their energies on strangers. Anyone who goes to the effort of working magic against you will have some kind of reason, and this usually falls into one of two categories: you have upset them in some way, or you have something they want quite badly. In other words, magical attacks are like any other form of personal violence, they usually come from someone you know, or think you know!

So, if you have reason to suspect that negative magic is being directed towards you, the next step is to take a long hard look at your recent activities to see if you can identify the person who may be upset with you and, if possible, try to put things right. This is not only in keeping with our belief in personal responsibility, it has the practical advantage of removing any desire they may have to repeat the spell! By the way, do not make the mistake of assuming that someone would not be able to work negative magic just because they have never shown any signs of being interested in the Craft, as many skilled magical practitioners, whether Witches or otherwise, do not advertise the fact! Of course you may not be able to be certain of the source of the magic, but it is worth trying to be sure.

Once you are sure that you are being attacked in this way, it obviously makes sense to renew your defensive boundaries, perhaps doing a cleansing first to be on the safe side. I would also strongly recommend placing a mirror in the window, facing the direction of the sender. After this is done, you can work to remove the problem, and if you are certain you know the sender then you can be fairly direct.

One of the most effective methods is to take two mirrors (the folding type intended to be carried in a handbag are good for this) and between them place a photo of the person in question. Around these tie a triple length of black thread. As you do so, visualize their negative magic being reflected back upon them. Be specific about this: it should be their negative magic, not all their magic, otherwise you leave them no room for personal growth. If you have no photograph, you could use a drawing or even a slip of paper with their personal information which you have formally Named through the Elements.

An equally effective method is to take a biggish flat stone. On one side you inscribe the name of the person, or a sigil to represent them, and on the other put a large equal-armed cross. It's worth remembering that the equal-armed cross vastly predates the Christian one and is not to be confused with it. Use a form of inscription which will not smudge when you later varnish it, like

the real witches' craft

enamel modelling paint, and black is the best colour. Once this has dried, the next steps should take place in the Circle. Tie a black thread around the stone so that it likewise forms a cross on both sides. Varnish the stone (quick drying clear nail varnish works well!) on both sides so that the whole is sealed and protected. You may find this quite tricky as obviously one side will still be sticky whilst you are doing the other. I have found that balancing it on edge, using some blutak, allows me to varnish both sides and if you pause half way down the height of the stone it is easy to turn it over as the top will dry fairly rapidly. Whilst doing this, visualize the symbol, the thread, and the varnish, all binding this person's negative magical intent. Once the stone is dry, pass it through each of the Elements in turn, calling upon them to prevent this person working against you. After your magic, put the stone away in a safe place and, this is important, do not tell anyone about it.

You should also check to see whether you have anything which might provide a tangible link with the person. This could be gifts from them, things which you have borrowed, or, in cases of extreme acrimony, something they have deliberately left in your home to create a link. In the case of anything you have borrowed, the solution is easy; return it soon as you can. Gifts are rather more complex; obviously, if you suddenly return a series of presents it will do nothing to foster harmony. The best solution is, perhaps oddly, to buy a gift in return. It does not have to be expensive, but should be selected with genuine care, so that it will be appreciated. By doing this you redress the balance between you and the other person, and this helps to negate the link. It is often said that you should be careful of receiving a gift from a Witch, because of its potential to be a magical link. However, if you always ensure that you respond with something of like value (as opposed to cost) then you will know that there is balance in your relationship. Having reciprocated, you should also then cleanse anything you have from them. If you still feel uncomfortable, you can get rid of those gifts, perhaps by donating them to a second-hand shop. Even if it is your intent from the outset to dispose of these presents, do cleanse them so that you are not potentially passing negativity onto an unsuspecting third party! If they have actually left something in your home, with the intention of forming a link, you will be able to trace this using the same technique as you did to locate negativity. Such items can then be cleansed and disposed of.

There is another technique you can use to try to identify the person working against you, and that is to visit the astral and to trace the thread of negative magic back to its source. However, this is not without its risks; if the person is more competent than you then they may become aware of your actions. Even if they are not, but are working on the astral when you come across them, you risk being noticed, which could result in them increasing their efforts. By now, I think you'll begin to see why battles of magic or Witch wars are so carefully avoided!

However, even if you have no idea who is directing negative magic in your direction, there is another form of spell you can use, although it is somewhat more complex. First, you need to find a smallish bottle, preferably one which is narrower at the neck than at its base. Then get a cork which either fits, or can be cut to fit, snugly. For the first step place some of your hair and nail clippings into the bottle. Traditionally, a Witch would have also added a couple of drops of their blood too, but it will work without. Do not seal the bottle yet. Name it, through the Elements, as yourself and to attract and draw all negative magics. Place it upright, somewhere safe, but outside of your defended area, for three whole days and nights. After the time has elapsed cast a protective Circle and only then go and collect the bottle, remembering to open and close a doorway in the Circle each time you leave or enter it. Take the bottle directly to the Circle and add seven new pins, then seal it with the cork and affix it with a little molten wax. In this way you will have captured the essence of the spell. Take a black thread and tie it around the bottle. It doesn't need to be tied in a cross form, around the neck will do. Then seal the knot with a few more drops of melted wax. Now pass the bottle through each of the Elements in turn, calling upon each to bind the spell. Complete your ritual in the usual way and then, as soon as you can, take the bottle out to a place well away from your home and bury it, deeply. Try to find somewhere

the real witches' craft

where it will remain undisturbed, as you don't want it found and opened, at least until the spell has run its natural course.

Once you have severed connections with the person who is working negatively against you, and cleansed and protected your home and family, life will return to normal. Usually, this will take place almost immediately, but just occasionally it may take longer. In this case, it is a good idea to take some time to work on balancing the Elements within yourself. Any form of negativity can result in us becoming less in balance than usual, more so if you feel you have been deliberately targeted. It's normal to feel hurt, offended, and to want to retaliate. However, for the reasons stated earlier we really shouldn't counter attack with attack. Whatever you may feel about the morality of it, the bottom line is that it is detrimental to our spiritual growth, and our own ability to work magic of any kind. You may come across the suggestion that you can use the curse: 'May they get what they truly deserve.' But even this should be used sparingly and with caution, as it's not without its potential to rebound or to work in a way you may not have foreseen. Besides, if you really want to get your own back on someone, then the very best thing is to be seen to be succeeding despite anything they might send your way!

CORRECTING MISTAKES

Negative spells are not the only ones you may want to stop. It's a rare Witch indeed who has never made a mistake, or wanted to put a halt to an otherwise effective spell. This could be for any number of reasons; perhaps more information has come to light, meaning that the spell should have been different, or the circumstances have changed. Possibly you've thought it through and think that your spell might not have the effect you intended. If you're working for someone else, they may have changed their mind. Whatever the cause, it's useful to know how to be able to stop or counter your own magic. There are two likely points at which you might want to do this; either during the magic, or after it has been sent. The former is relatively

the darker side of magic

simple, the latter slightly more complex, but in either case the important thing is to remain calm and focused. I can remember what it feels like to suddenly think, 'Oh no! That isn't what I intended at all!' and to feel a level of panic rising, but if you give way to this you don't have the control necessary to put things right.

If you are in the middle of a working and decide, for some reason, that you don't want or need to continue, then all you have to do is to stop and to reverse the steps you have taken so far. This means releasing any power raised; into the earth, or into the water on your Altar, banishing the Elements and thanking the Goddess and the God. If you have created any object, like a talisman or a fith-fath, then this should be destroyed. Or if you have consecrated an object which you don't wish to destroy then this will need to be thoroughly cleansed and then blessed in a neutral manner.

However, should the energy have already been released and the spell sent on its way then you will need to assess how best to stop or undo it. Stopping a spell will have the effect of leaving things as they are, with such effects as have taken place being unchanged. Undoing a spell means that you may have to work another spell in order to return things to the way they were before. Only try to undo a spell if it's actually essential, considering whether any changes can be left in place without detriment. If you really do think that it has to be undone, then you will need to go back to the original steps of assessing not only the new spell, but also its side effects. Also spend some time in meditation prior to your working, thinking about the situation as you thought of it at the time of your first spell, and as it now is, for you don't want to make any additional changes, other than to reverse the effects of the spell.

Assuming you kept full notes on your magic in your journal or Book of Shadows you will have the detail on how you constructed the magic, which will help you to undo it; otherwise you will have to do the best you can from memory. Where you used any kind of tangible object in the original, this can

the real witches' craft

be taken into the Circle and the magic removed by passing it through each of the Elements in turn, asking them to remove the spell and return things to the way they were. Where the original spell was performed with no tangible object, then the most logical thing to do is to reverse each step in turn, or to create a new spell.

Consideration of how we can correct our spells and magic brings us back to where we started in this book, in that it is important that we do the groundwork first in order to direct the energy we have raised into the solutions we actually need. As I, and many others have said, so many times before; be careful what you wish for, as you just might get it.

INDEX

index

the real witches' craft

Also by Kate West

Real Witchcraft: an Introduction, co-written with David Williams, 1996. Reprinted 2003 by I-H-O Books, Mandrake Press. A basic introduction to the Craft.

Pagan Rites of Passage, Mandrake Press, 1997. A series of booklets giving information and Rituals for the Rites of Passage of Handfasting, Naming, the Rites of Withdrawal, and the Rites of Aging.

The Real Witches' Handbook, Thorsons, HarperCollins, 2000. Real Witchcraft for real people with real lives; this book shows how to practise the Craft in a way sensitive to those around you.

The Real Witches' Kitchen, Thorsons, HarperCollins, 2002. Oils, lotions and ointments for Magic and to relieve and heal. Soaps and bathing distillations for Circle and Magical work. Magical incenses, candles and sachets to give or to keep. Food and drink to celebrate the Sabbats, for personal well-being and to share with friends.

A Spell in your Pocket, Element Books, HarperCollins, 2002. A handy pocket-sized gift book for the Witch on the move.

The Real Witches' Coven, Element Books, HarperCollins, 2003. A complete guide to running a Coven. Problems and solutions, and real-life examples of what can, and does, happen in a Coven. For the new, or would-be, High Priestess and/or High Priest this covers all the aspects you need to know. For the experienced High Priestess/High Priest, there are new insights and stories you will relate too. For the would-be Coven member, this tells you what to expect!

The Real Witches' Book of Spells and Rituals, Element Books, HarperCollins, 2003. Spells for all occasions, Rituals for seasonal festivals, Rites of Passage and Initiations, and much more.

The Real Witches' Garden, Element Books, HarperCollins, 2004. Ways of using your garden to enhance your Craft, and your Craft to enhance the garden. Whether your contact with nature is a windowsill or an acre, here are ways of getting closer to nature and unlocking the magical power of the land.

The Real Witches' Year, Element Books, HarperCollins, 2005. Brings real magic into your life every day of the Year. Charms, spells, things to do, to learn and to make. A feast of Wiccan Lore.

Elements of Chants, Pyewacket Productions, 2005. Produced by Steve Paine. A CD lasting over an hour. Wiccan chants and spoken ritual pieces, created, sung and spoken by Kate and her Coven the Hearth of Hecate. These are available from the Children of Artemis, www.witchcraft.org.